IN HER OWN RITE

CONSTRUCTING FEMINIST LITURGICAL TRADITION

Pastor Cleoramae graper

8 June 1990

Elisabeth Sace

MARJORIE PROCTER-SMITH

IN HER OWN RITE

CONSTRUCTING FEMINIST LITURGICAL TRADITION

ABINGDON PRESS

Nashville

In Her Own Rite:
Constructing Feminist Liturgical Tradition

This book is printed on acid-free paper.

Library of Congress Cataloging-in-Publication Data

Procter-Smith, Marjorie
  In her own rite: constructing feminist liturgical tradition/
  Marjorie Procter-Smith.
    p. cm.
  Includes bibliographical references.
  ISBN 0-687-18787-7 (alk. paper)
  1. Liturgics. 2. Feminist theology. I. Title
  BV178.P76 1990   89-28410
  264'.0082—dc20   CIP

Scripture quotations in this publication unless otherwise noted are from the
Revised Standard Version of the Bible, copyrighted 1946, 1952, © 1971, 1973
by the Division of Christian Education of the National Council of the Churches
of Christ in the U.S.A., and are used by permission.

The lines from "Transcendental Etude" (pp. 49, 66), "Hunger" (p. 163), and
"Natural Resources" (p. 171) from *The Dream of Common Language, Poems
1974–1977* by Adrienne Rich are used with permission of the author and W.
W. Norton and Company, Inc. Copyright © 1978 by W. W. Norton and
Company, Inc.

The lines from "The Images" (pp. 13, 91, 115) and "Integrity" (p. 170), from *A
Wild Patience Has Taken Me This Far, Poems 1978–1981* by Adrienne Rich are
used with the permission of the author and W. W. Norton and Company, Inc.
Copyright © 1981 by Adrienne Rich.

The excerpt from page 170 is reprinted with permission of Collier Books, an
imprint of Macmillan Publishing Company, from *For Colored Girls Who Have
Considered Suicide When the Rainbow is Enuf* by Ntozake Shange. Copyright ©
1975, 1976, 1977 by Ntozake Shange.

MANUFACTURED IN THE UNITED STATES OF AMERICA

IN MEMORIAM

Marjorie Fredericks Procter
August 30, 1916–January 11, 1960

CONTENTS

INTRODUCTION

T he purpose of this book is exploration. As a feminist and a student of liturgy and a teacher of worship, I have long been conscious of the cognitive dissonance between the commitments and values of the liturgical movement on the one hand and those of the feminist movement on the other. Feminist friends want to know "what's a good feminist like you doing in a field like liturgical studies?" Colleagues in liturgical studies regard my interest in feminist thought as extrinsic or irrelevant to liturgical work. Although at times the dissonance has been subdued, of late I have been more and more aware of a need to bring, if not exactly harmony, at least an antiphonal, dialogical quality to the existence of these two important contemporary movements. This book has been brought into being by a desire to explore the possibilities of common ground and to identify areas of disagreement in order to begin a dialogue between feminism and liturgical studies.

The presupposition of this book is bold. It proceeds from what some will regard as an unwarranted assumption that such common ground exists and that dialogue is therefore possible. For me, no other position is feasible at present. By training and by personal inclination and conviction I am persuaded that the liturgical movement, at its best, has the potential for reforming the church of our day as dramatically as did the reformations of earlier centuries. I am convinced that such reformation is badly needed and will bear much fruit. On the other hand, I am always aware of the oppression of women in a patriarchal church and society. I am always aware that the world is not safe for women. Women are abused, achieve too little, and die too young. I am also aware of the church's uneasy complicity in that suffering, and I am always appalled by the needlessness of it. I am convinced that the feminist movement is causing a change of profound significance for the church's future. I am further convinced that to enable that movement is to hasten the church's healing and the healing of the church's witness to the world.

This bold assumption is not, however, merely an effort to relieve my own tensions over my discordant commitments. It is rather motivated by a desire to offer the gifts and insights of each movement to the other out of a twofold commitment to the church and to the women of the church. I am convinced that the combination of these two forces can initiate a profound change for the good in the church's identity and its mission, a change that must come if the church is to survive into the next century as a viable witness to the gospel. The reader must judge on the basis of what follows in the chapters of this book whether this assumption is warranted.

The contents are in some ways preliminary. Chapter 1 identifies some of the common ground that exists between feminism and the liturgical movement. The next chapter proposes a framework for taking up some of the basic issues which emerge and attempts to generate a feminist liturgical method for the purposes of interpretation. A valid liturgical method, it has been argued, must first attend to the function of liturgy, mindful that liturgy is rich and complex, and capable of expressing more than one meaning.[1] So I have identified what must surely be foundational to liturgical events in a Christian context: memory and imagination. A sound feminist method concerns itself with women's experience and with viewing a given subject or event through women's eyes. The resonances of these two actions, to remember and to imagine, are explored for women, who occupy a particular location in our society and in the church.

The following chapters, too, are exploratory and preliminary—or perhaps "primary" in the sense of "beginning." I have identified the issues which seem to me to be most basic. Basic issues for the women's movement have been language about people and language and images for God (chapters 3 and 4). Feminists and liturgical scholars meet in mutual concern over the problem of the role of the Bible in liturgy and the nature of preaching (chapter 5).

Chapter 6 takes up what have been largely liturgical concerns, the sacraments of baptism and eucharist, in order to explore feminist liturgical perspectives on these formative Christian acts. The final chapter deals with developing feminist liturgical spirituality and addresses the relationship between liturgy and life from a feminist perspective.

Certainly much is left unaddressed by this book. The pressing and important question of ordination is set aside here, chiefly because it has generated such a large body of literature already that I am reluctant to add to it. The reader will perceive that the pages that follow assume full participation of women in liturgical presidency, and are less concerned with defending the practice in the abstract than with exploring its possibilities in connection with actual liturgical acts. But certainly there is room for much more reflection on the significance of women's liturgical presidency than is presently available. The same holds true for women as preachers. Related questions of leadership and authority also deserve further development.[2]

Especially important, and largely unexplored in these pages, is the recovery of women's liturgical history. A thorough reconsideration of women's liturgical roles and participation using feminist methods of retrieval and interpretation is called for. In particular, I am painfully aware of the absence in this study of serious invocation of our foresisters of the nineteenth-century women's movement, many of whom addressed some of the same questions that have motivated the writing of this book. I grieve over this gap in my education, and I am aware that if we knew our own history as women better, there would be less need to keep doing some of the same work over and over again.

Examples could be multiplied, and no doubt the reader will be able to supply a full list of unaddressed topics. But this is exactly as it should be. This book is preliminary in precisely this sense. If others find here directions, implications, and/or impulses for further work, this book will have achieved its purpose.

Although this book is a product of my own work, and I accept responsibility for its weaknesses as well as it strengths, I have been helped by many in the writing of it. Students in my classes at Perkins School of Theology have asked the right questions and provoked me into asking yet more questions. The students in my class on Liturgy and Women's Experience at the Social Justice Institute in Edmonton, Alberta, Canada, were prime movers in the writing of this book, since they knew I was going to write it before I did. In a way, it is really their book.

I am grateful to Davis Perkins, formerly of Abingdon Press, who responded to my proposal for this book with enthusiasm and support, and to Ulrike Guthrie, who has edited and shepherded the manuscript with grace and good will. Ann Ralston patiently typed and retyped the manuscript, corrected misspellings, and caught many errors.

My valued colleagues in the Feminist Liturgy Working Group of the North American Academy of Liturgy gave time, energy, constructive criticism, and enthusiasm to a discussion of the project. Carol Adams, Janet Walton, Mary Collins, Kathleen Hughes, and Teresa Mallott read and commented on early drafts with careful and critical eyes. Although I did not take all of their suggestions, the book is undoubtedly better for those I did take.

I am blessed with a generous and supportive family. Sterling Procter provided shelter and comforting food during the writing of several chapters. Jeremy Procter-Smith continues to model the kind of perseverance in the face of difficulty which is necessary not only to writing books but also to creating the kind of changes this book is about. George Procter-Smith is the true midwife of this book. He did proofreading and editing, but (more significantly) he literally made the writing of this book possible and the ideas in it believable by demonstrating what it means to be a woman-identified man.

This book is dedicated to the memory of my mother, a valiant woman.

Marjorie Procter-Smith
Perkins School of Theology
Southern Methodist University
Dallas, Texas
Saint Brigid's Day, 1989

CHAPTER ONE

"ARE THEY TRUE FOR US?"

Feminism and Christian Liturgy

In her poem "The Images," Adrienne Rich laments the power of humanly created forms such as language, music, and art to disguise and to mystify oppression, to "reorganize victimization," "translating violence into patterns so powerful and pure / we continually fail to ask are they true for us."[1] It is this fundamental truth-question which motivates this beginning dialogue between feminist theology and liturgical theology.

Liturgy is certainly a humanly created form that is both powerful and pure. It is the result of a many-centuried process of encounter between God and human communities gathered together again and again in a particular but ever-changing historical context. Because liturgy is the evidence of this living process, it makes claims of truth. To be precise, the liturgy claims that when its work is being done, participants are engaging in a dialogue with God. The claim of encounter with God gives the liturgical event its power and its truth. Liturgical "truth," then, is not at all an abstract or purely intellectual truth, but an engaged, embodied, and particular truth, a truth that cannot only be talked about, but must be done.

But now a new question must be asked of the liturgy and its claims to truth: is it true for us? Is liturgy one of the "forms created" indicted by Rich for their ability to "reorganize victimization"? Does the liturgy "translate violence" into beautiful forms, disguising its danger for women? The truth-question that Rich asks is also not abstract; it is a question about what is true *for us,* for women living in these times. And if the liturgy claims to reflect centuries of dialogue and

13

relationship between God and people, to what extent does it reflect the full participation of women in that dialogue and relationship? Or is our exclusion from the dialogue part of the process of our victimization? And if women have indeed been excluded from the dialogue, what will happen when we join it? That women intend to join the dialogue is evident on all sides. Theological discussions about scripture, tradition, history, and the fundamentals of the faith are slowly becoming discussions that are increasingly able to take account, at last, of women's experience, history, and lives. Women have begun to enter into that most foundational of theological dialogues, the liturgical one, as the publication of feminist liturgical resources and the ongoing discussion about the use of inclusive language in prayers and hymns demonstrate.

Our entry into this dialogue has been motivated by a sense of disaffection with traditional liturgy. Although the issue of inclusive language has received the greatest amount of public attention, the critique goes much deeper. Evident in many of the alternative liturgies produced by the feminist movement are a profound sense of betrayal by the church and grief for the loss of history and tradition. This sense of betrayal and loss is often expressed in the creation of litanies of names of women forgotten or misrepresented by traditional liturgies. We have entered this dialogue out of a desire to end the silence imposed on women in the church and on our traditions and our memories. What have we said? What have been our contributions to the liturgical dialogue?

THE FEMINIST CRITIQUE OF PATRIARCHY

Feminists have pointed out ways in which the very nature of the dialogue has been shaped by the reality of patriarchal society and church. Defining patriarchy, as a male colleague once observed, is like a fish trying to define water. It is, he perceived, so much the natural environment in which we all live that it is almost impossible for us to see it. Yet if patriarchy is the water in which we live, then the water is toxic, especially for women and for many men who are non-white, non-Western, or non-wealthy.

Patriarchy is a complex social structure built on the simple premise that only the free, propertied male is the citizen. Within such a structure, women, children, and slaves have no civil status of their own; such status as they do have is derived from that of the free male to whose household they belong. Terms such as father, husband, master, wife, son, daughter, and slave define patriarchal relationships within a patriarchal household. The father/husband/master, as the normative citizen, is "head" of this household. The traditional biblical concern for "the widow and the orphan" (where "fatherless" is a synonym for "orphan") is a recognition by patriarchal society that the husbandless woman and fatherless child are entirely without power, status, or resources. They are dependent on the good will of society. The society on which they are dependent, of course, is the same one which has deprived them of independent status and means. Any aid that they receive from society thus must maintain their dependent status, since to alter the status of the woman or child would threaten patriarchal social structures themselves. The woman with no male "head" as father, husband, or master must remain anomalous in patriarchal society, an object of pity, scorn, or fear, or perhaps simply not seen, but never a person of status or identity.

Among men, status is distinguished by class, wealth, family connections, race, or profession. Thus some men rule not only over women and children, but also over men of lesser power and lower status. The result is a pyramidal structure with a few males at the top and the many with lesser or no status—women, children, and most men—at the bottom.

Since the plausibility of such a social system is by no means self-evident, myriad means of maintenance and reinforcement are required to keep it in place. A foundational element in this effort is the idea of androcentrism. If the free male is the normative citizen in a patriarchal social/political system, the male human must be the normative human being in the accompanying system of ideas and values. If the male is the normative human being, the measure of all things, the female must at best be derivative and secondary, at worst abnormal and dangerous or fearsome. The man is human; the woman must be "Other." Moreover, if the male human is the normative human, the existence of the female then must be explained and defined in terms that make her different from the male. Since in fact the physiological differences between male and female are minor, they must be magnified, emphasized, and made into the whole definition of woman. So the woman is defined by her childbearing function and sexuality. Female sexuality and maternity, as defined by patriarchy, are simultaneously sources of women's identities and signs of their inherent weaknesses, and are to be regarded with a measure of fear and revulsion by men and women alike. Women's own experiences of their sexuality and maternity, as perhaps including delight, awe, or joy, are excluded from the definition.

Androcentric reality is constructed and sustained by the subtle means of symbols and language. Language that reflects the assumption that the male is the norm, that "man" means "person" and "person" means "man," renders women invisible or marginal. Linguistically, women appear as exceptions or problems. Symbolically, women represent sexuality, maternity, and thus perhaps physicality, nature, and natural processes. The indifference of natural processes to patriarchal definitions and structure is defined as anarchy and thus something to be controlled and subdued, to be "mastered," as women, children, and lower-status men must be. Allowing only men into the public sphere has symbolic as well as political consequences. The male presence—voice, body, manner—becomes the "representative" and "public" person, a figure capable of bearing the weight of representing the human race or some smaller collectivity which includes, even if marginally, women and children. The female presence in the public sphere in anything other than a supportive role is rendered illegitimate. A female figure in an androcentric environment cannot bear the symbolic weight of representing the entire human race, in spite of the fact that women in reality do bear the entire human race. A "public woman" is a prostitute. A woman who claims a place in the public sphere creates symbolic dissonance; she must be a "bad" woman, because a "good" woman is by definition marginal, supportive, silent, and invisible.

Together with androcentrism in supporting a patriarchal social system are the ideas of racism, classism, and ageism. Since economic advantage and access to power are more available to some men than to others in a patriarchal system, these same men, who are white, English-speaking, upper-class, and neither too young nor too old, are valued above other men and all women and children. As in the androcentric world view, those who do not fall into this category of valued men are defined as deficient or illegitimate in some sense. They are at least not normative or representative, and are often regarded as mentally or emotionally incompetent, or of poor or unreliable character. Indeed, many of the same characteristics of emotionalism, irrationality, and lower mental ability are applied to women and to non-white people as a whole. Similarly, the comparison of women and non-whites to children reveals the low status of children as well as of those who are being compared to children. Thus one's status and value in a patriarchal society are determined not only by one's sex, but also by race, ethnicity, age, and class.

The attribution of devalued characteristics to women and other oppressed groups becomes part of androcentric anthropology, which defines such characteristics as part of our "nature." Such an anthropology then justifies both external and internal controls on women's behavior, "for our own good." These controls may be either restrictive or punitive, and operate at both an external and an internal level. External restrictions may be overt, such as denial of access to education, work, health care, or adequate pay for work. Punitive controls may even be brutal, as in the case of rape, battering, or sexual harassment. They may also be subtle, in language and other symbolic systems that are male-centered. Internal restrictions, self-imposed, are the result of external restrictions. In part the internalization of androcentric anthropology indicates acceptance of androcentric norms and thus self-devaluation and even self-hatred. But self-imposed controls are also a response to and a defense against external controls, which, as noted, can be brutal and even life-threatening. Hence some internalization of androcentric norms can be regarded as self-protective, though never life-enchancing.

Essential to the maintenance of a patriarchal structure, in addition to androcentrism, racism, classism, and ageism, is the ordering of all relationships into patterns of dominance and submission. There are not only interlocking patterns of valued people and unvalued people, but the valued people are assumed to possess the right to dominate those less valued. The corollary is that those less valued are expected to submit to "their betters." All of the above mentioned means of control, both punitive and restrictive, overt and subtle, are available to the dominant person or group in order to extract submission from others. Not only are the more valued people granted the right to dominate; those who are not valued are expected to submit "for their own good." In the case of temporary occasions of submission—in the case of a white male worker to a white boss, for example—the submission is justified by appeals to expediency, efficiency, or "the team spirit." But from some groups—women, children, people of color—submission before dominant white males is always demanded. In these cases, it is argued that it is in their nature to submit, even to desire it—they are "natural slaves."

THE FEMINIST LITURGICAL MOVEMENT

As a challenge to this patriarchal context, the feminist contribution to the liturgical dialogue is concerned with two issues: the question of memory, which is a question about history and tradition, and the question of imagination, which is a question about the future. About memory we say that the names and deeds of women have been forgotten, or their memories distorted. We have wanted to reinterpret and reclaim women who have been remembered but whose memories have been used against us, such as Eve and Lilith.[2] We have also reinterpreted and reclaimed pre-Christian and non-Christian traditions which seem to be more attentive to and respectful of women's experience and memory. This is particularly evident in the reconstruction of a feminist religion that worships a Goddess, but this search for a feminist religious tradition has influenced Christian feminism also.[3]

About imagination, we say that our ability to imagine a future church in which women are not silent and marginal has been constricted. Our ability to imagine God as anything other than an old man, or to imagine our selves, women and men, as free and mutually empowering people, has been constricted. Our imaginations (and not just women's) have been colonized. Claiming alternative interpretations of the past and of our traditions helps free our imaginations, as has the recovery (or reconstruction) of Goddess-worship as a living practice. Feminist liturgies are not simply backward-looking, but are generating new models for the church and new images of God, of humanity, and of the church's relationship with God and with the world. Feminist liturgies are always in some sense prophetic, endeavoring, as Arlene Swidler says, "to present to their faith communities a vision of the way things can be in the future."[4]

Of course, in this primary theological dialogue, it is not only the church with which we are conversing. Although the church's conversation with itself on matters such as those outlined above is critical to its identity, this is not the fundamental business of liturgy. Liturgy, as noted above, is essentially encounter with the One who gathers the people together and who acts in the midst of and through the assembly. The visible, vocal entry of women into the public enactment of business with God is what concerns us here because it is what concerns the church's liturgy. So the questions raised by women about memory and imagination call for a transformation of that relationship between God and community. If liturgy is indeed not only *about* God but *of* God, as Aidan Kavanagh urges, then the feminist critique challenges more than the church's identity and self-understanding. It also challenges the relationship between God and the church, and brings a new level of discourse to that relationship.[5]

The feminist movement is not the only current movement to challenge the relationship between God and the church, or to suggest that the relationship has become distorted and unauthentic. The liturgical movement, which began over one hundred years before the feminist liturgical movement, is challenging the way the church engages in its public worship of God. Like the present feminist liturgical movement, the liturgical movement from its beginnings in the 1830s was concerned not only that the church's liturgy was diminishing the church's ability to witness to the gospel in the world and distorting the church's sense of identity, but also, and more fundamentally, that poor liturgy endangered the church's authentic relationship with God.[6] Unlike the feminist liturgical movement, the liturgical movement has focused energy on recovering liturgical practices of the church's past, at first of the medieval period, later of the early church, as a means of restoring integrity to the church's liturgy.

It is worth noting, by way of contrast, that the liturgical movement was initiated and led by educated European men who were often members of the clergy. Although the movement initially experienced criticism and rejection from the church hierarchy, and its ideas were discredited for a time, its ultimate success and dissemination across denominations and continents was undoubtedly aided by the fact that its leaders were people of power and authority in the church. The feminist liturgical movement encounters resistance not only to its ideas because they challenge prevailing assumptions about liturgy and church, but also to its leaders because they are women.

Although the critique of contemporary patterns and habits of worship offered by the liturgical movement was threatening to church hierarchy, it was a critique based on historical norms. It did not challenge the validity of the church's tradition itself, but rather called the present church into closer conformity with what were understood to be the authentic patterns and practices of the church of an earlier age. It would be inaccurate, however, to see the liturgical movement as attempting to return to the past or to recreate the past in the present. At its best, the movement attempts to restate liturgical norms which emerge from the historical study of liturgy so that they may be reappropriated for the renewal of the contemporary church.

Aside from the differences in the social location of the leaders of the two movements, it is evident that there are significant differences in values and commitments between the two. The liturgical movement searches out liturgical norms from the church's liturgical practices of the past. On the other hand, the feminist liturgical movement is deeply suspicious of the past as traditionally interpreted, aware of the silencing and marginalizing of women in the construction of tradition, and wishes instead to develop norms out of women's experience. Is genuine dialogue possible between two movements which seem to be moving resolutely in different directions, or at least toward different goals? I believe it is possible, and moreover that such dialogue will be fruitful to both movements.

A necessary prerequisite to dialogue, however, is the discovery of some common ground, and we now turn our attention to this effort. We will examine the basic values and assumptions of each movement, which may reveal not only areas of common commitment but also areas of possible fruitful dialogue and mutual enrichment.

Because the feminist liturgical movement is relatively new on the scene (originating in the early 1970s), and because theoretical work on it has only begun, generalizing about its values and assumptions must remain somewhat tentative. Also, it should be noted that although a good number of feminist liturgies have come into print since 1970 probably the majority are unpublished by intention. While this makes general comments more difficult, it also reveals significant values held by some of the women involved in creating and participating in such events.[7]

The value expressed in a reluctance to publish liturgies may be characterized as a commitment to *contextuality*. Feminist liturgies and rituals are often understood to be non-transferable to other gatherings or other occasions; they arise out of the particularities of the praying community or in response to a particular need or situation. They are also contextual in the sense that they take seriously the social and political context of the community. Thus liturgies designed for use with women's gatherings may be felt to be inappropriate for use in mixed groups or for groups of men. Collections of feminist liturgies which are published commonly include assertions that the book is to be used as "an idea-book, a mind-opener," as one editor put it. The liturgies are definitely not to be "replayed" for different communities; they are rather to serve as examples or models, or even as moments in a larger process into which the reader is invited.[8] The editors of another collection expressed it even more sharply:

> *This book is a mirror and not a picture.* It is written to ask questions and to point toward ways of asking them, not to provide answers. Particular images of God, and particular worship forms and the theological assumptions on which these images stand, will arise from the answers of each group of users. Those answers recorded in the handbook itself are a set of responses that a once-in-a-lifetime, never-to-be-reconstituted group arrived at with joy and some pain. They belong to no one else. Their greatest value will lie in the stimulation they provide to pursue the search.[9]

Reluctance to publish feminist liturgies arises in part, therefore, from a conviction that they belong to the group that created and participated in them, and "to no one else."

A related concern evident in the collections and in the reluctance to publish is the commitment to process. Writers reflecting on a given liturgy remark that the process of creating it was at least as important as the liturgical event itself. This experience is particularly intense if the liturgies were created out of a group process. The mixture of joy and pain noted in the quotation above is echoed throughout the published commentaries on the liturgies, with the process most often described as "struggle." The process serves as a kind of *conscientization* as planners attempt to express in word and ritual act the complex experience of being Christian and feminist.

One also notes a firm commitment to experimentality. This is not, however, an experimentality which is born of a casual or careless attitude about liturgy. It is quite the opposite. It is motivated instead by a conviction that liturgy is of utmost importance and by a sense of modesty about what is possible at the present time. "These liturgies are not finished products but just steps along an unending path," notes one editor.[10] Commentators frequently express a sense of dissatisfaction with the finished liturgy, a sense that the process of exploration of this uncharted territory has only begun. There is the haunting feeling that the goal has not only not been reached, but that it perhaps is not even visible yet. As one commentator put it, in attempting to describe the kind of seder to which she would like to take her as yet unborn children, "for me it has not yet crystallized."[11]

These three values—contextuality, commitment to process, and experimentality—give feminist liturgical events a character which is distinctive. The liturgies are usually created for a very specific and sometimes concrete reason, such as a healing service for a rape victim or to celebrate the opening of a women's center. Thus they tend to have a clear purpose and are motivated by real needs. Explanations about why they are necessary are generally not needed. This common sense of purpose also fosters a level of intense engagement with the liturgical event in the participants that traditional churches might envy.

Two other interrelated values are present in these liturgies. There is explicit rejection of hierarchical forms of liturgical leadership and a corresponding commitment to shared leadership. This is expressed in the preference for communally generated liturgies (and the emphasis on process). It is also expressed in the style of leadership used, in the desire to enable maximum participation on the part of the worshipers, in the ritual forms preferred (litanies, spontaneous prayers, congregational responses to sermons, readings, etc.), and in the way space is arranged and used (a preference for flexible space and circular arrangements).[12]

The last value which will concern us here is difficult to label; it is something between pluralism and ecumenicity as those terms are normally used, but neither catches it exactly. It can perhaps better be described than labeled. It is evident in Arlene Swidler's 1974 collection of feminist liturgies, which contains the following:

1. A Protestant liturgy used at Princeton Theological Seminary Chapel;

2. A Mother's Day liturgy used on two occasions at Graduate Theological Union, designed by a class;

3. *Brit Kedusha,* a Jewish ceremony for celebrating the birth of a daughter;

4. A Mass for freedom for women;

5. A Celebration for the opening of the Ecumenical Women's Centers;

6. An ecumenical liturgy celebrating the fifty-third anniversary of women's suffrage, which is biblical in content but not exclusively Christian;

7. A service of exorcism remembering the women burned as witches, used on Halloween;

8. A Mother's Day service based on the framework of the Episcopal liturgy;

9. A Jewish women's Hagada.

Certainly there is pluralism here, and in some cases ecumenicity too. But more fundamentally there is the sense that a commonality exists among women which transcends, even if momentarily, the literally man-made distinctions of religious, traditional, or confessional barriers. As Esther M. Broner observes, "We were women before we were Jews, Christians, Moslems. It seems only natural, historical, and just, therefore, to make religion respond to our origins."[13] The comfort with which the liturgies coexist in Swidler's collection, the ease with which feminists borrow freely from one another's traditions and generate liturgies which can be used in gatherings of Christians, or Jews, or neo-pagans may seem to contradict the values discussed above in connection with contextuality, but in fact it reflects a conviction that our experiences as women provide the necessary common ground for such borrowing and sharing.[14] Rosemary Ruether notes, "It has become common at such gatherings of Christian women that ideas drawn from feminist Judaism or the Goddess movement might also be employed in liturgy."[15]

In gatherings of women, then, denominational, confessional, or traditional divisions are relativized. In large part this is due to the conviction (or hope) that behind or beneath the patriarchal traditions of present-day religions lie options, if not actual traditions, which are woman-identified or gynocentric. The search for and construction of a non-patriarchal religion is seen as a common endeavor. The goal, however, is not (at least at present) a single uniform feminist religion, but the transformation of the existing religious traditions of which women are already a part. This process of transformation, which has empowered women to name our own experiences, has revealed the complexity and the particularity of that experience. Women of color especially have challenged the tendency of white women to attempt to speak for all women, and have begun to name the reality of racism and classism among women.

THE LITURGICAL MOVEMENT

As indicated above, the liturgical movement is a much more influential movement in the present-day churches, in part due to its longevity, in part because it has generated a vast body of research and publication, and in part because its leaders have been men who have access to or are part of church hierarchies. Since the liturgical movement itself has been the object of much research and its ideas are widely available, our discussion of the values and goals of this movement will be presented in somewhat summary fashion. Moreover, as resources for this summary, we shall take, not the ideas of the movement's leaders (although these would offer an interesting perspective), but the liturgical results of the movement in the production of reformed liturgies for the church's use. Not only may we thereby acknowledge that there may be a gap between the ideas of a movement's leaders and the carrying out of those ideas in actual situations, but we also get a better parallel with the feminist liturgical movement, which has thus far not concerned itself very much with theory and research.

Of course, even in choosing to focus on the actual liturgies produced for particular faith communities significant assymetry between the two movements is made apparent. The liturgies generated as a result of the liturgical movement are the product of long processes, marked by the careful research, consultation, and evaluation that are possible with the financial support of the denomination. Publication of these commissions' efforts was assured, and wide dissemination and discussion are an inevitable part of the process (although they are not, of course, protected from controversy). The products of the feminist liturgical movement invariably have the ad hoc character of liturgies produced in the absence of financial support, institutional commitment, or assurance of publication.

Common to all denominations engaged in the process of liturgical reform has been a preoccupation with norms. Liturgical change is recognized as threatening to many in the church, and thus, proposed new rites often include careful statements about the reasons for the changes and the way in which they were conceived. The process of critique of existing liturgical practices began in response to several forces. First, there was the advance in understanding of the worship of the early, pre-Trent, pre-Reformation church produced by the increase in scholarship on this subject. Such research put into sharper perspective the limitations of patterns inherited from periods when the pastoral demands on the liturgy were much different than they are today. Second, there was in some communities a growing dissatisfaction on the part of clergy and people with certain aspects of the traditional forms, such as archaic or unintelligible language, inflexible forms, or perceived irrelevance to contemporary life. Third, there was a generalized sense that the church, as it moved into the twentieth century, was in need of a fundamental renewal of spirit and purpose if it were to survive into the twenty-first century. The means for this renewal was liturgical renewal.

We may identify, with James White, three norms which have shaped the work of liturgical renewal in recent times: *the historical norm, the theological norm,* and *the pastoral norm.*[16] *The historical norm* may fairly be said to be the foundational norm. The conviction that the practice of the ancient church, insofar as we can recover it, is not only relativizing but normative for current practice is evident to some degree in all reformed rites. In particular, the unity of word and sacrament in the Sunday service, the "four-fold" eucharistic action, and the "new emphasis on thanksgiving and praise" reflect "the influence of some of the earliest liturgies in the Christian community."[17] Appropriation of these ancient practices is regarded as desirable because it strengthens the Christian community's sense of identity.

The theological norm is often expressed in connection with statements about the historical norm. As the United Methodist resource *Word and Table* notes, "The restoration of the unified liturgy of the early churches . . . brings forth new theological understandings."[18] Where previous liturgical practices were regarded as being theologically weak or as distorting central theological principles of the church, liturgical renewal is concerned also to strengthen and correct. The church's liturgy is seen as a primary locus of theology, wherein theological doctrines or convictions are expressed and upheld.

The pastoral norm is concerned with the church as occupying a particular place in time and in society. Thus the church's liturgy must take account both of the needs of the worshiping community for a faith that is relevant to their lives and also of the church's need to witness to the world of the present day. This norm may act as a relativizing force on the historical norm, as the commentators on the Presbyterian *Service for the Lord's Day* observe:

> Apostolic, patristic, and Reformation precedent provide historical support for the pattern of Sunday worship provided in this order. However, the situations confronting the church in ancient and Reformation times were not identical with those that confront us today. The difference needs to be considered when adapting the old rites for our own use.[19]

However, more often the pastoral norm is regarded as being consistent with the historical norm. The same commentary notes, "The primary concern involved in the reform of worship life is that our worship may have integrity and be an instrument whereby the Holy Spirit strengthens our union with Christ and engages us in ministry."[20]

Thus a major characteristic of the liturgical movement is a concern for norms. Ideally, the historical, theological, and pastoral norms are to inform and balance one another.

> The continuing Liturgical Movement is part of the reawakening of the church. It seeks a recovery of those norms of liturgical worship of the Bible and the early church which lie behind Reformation divisions and medieval distortions, and which are fundamental to Christian liturgy in every time and place. It aims, however, not at an attempt to resuscitate the liturgy of the early church in the twentieth century, but at the restatement of the fundamentals in forms and expressions which can enable the liturgy to be the living prayer and work of the church today.[21]

As the above quotation indicates, two terms often used to describe the work of the movement are biblical and ecumenical. The concern for the appropriate use of Scripture is related to the question of norms, but tempered by the recognition that the Bible itself provides no liturgical patterns for Christian worship. Nevertheless, the liturgical movement has had a great influence on the churches' use of Scripture in liturgy by encouraging the reading and preaching of Scripture and above all by the creation of lectionary systems for such liturgical reading and preaching. In both Catholic and Protestant churches this has resulted in a renewed emphasis on biblical preaching. The production of lectionary-based homiletical and educational resources has placed much more of the Bible before the people than was common before the publication of these materials. This use of Scripture is distinctly liturgical, however. Scripture texts are selected according to the theological emphases of the season or feast of the church year (another significant concern of the liturgical movement).

Although ecumenicity has not been a primary goal of the liturgical movement, it has certainly been a happy result. The recovery of liturgical norms based on scholarship has become increasingly ecumenical and derives from a period of the church's life that predates many of the controversies that have divided us. Thus the recovery of liturgical norms has made sharing of liturgical resources inevitable. The commentator on the Presbyterian reformed rite puts it this way: "With the recovery of the Word-Sacrament shape as normative, we children of Calvin rejoin the ecumenical tradition and orient ourselves toward the coming of the unity of the church and the rule of Christ."[22]

A further characteristic that will concern us here is the emphasis on the liturgy as the work of the people. As commonly used and understood, this means that the liturgy is not the property or even the work of the ordained clergy but of the assembled faithful. The term most frequently used for this is taken from *The Constitution on the Sacred Liturgy.*

> Mother Church earnestly desires that all the faithful should be led to that full, conscious, and active participation in liturgical celebrations which is demanded by the very nature of the liturgy, and to which the Christian people, "a chosen race, a royal priesthood, a holy nation, a redeemed people" (I Peter 2:9, 4-5) have a right and obligation by reason of their baptism. In the restoration and promotion of the sacred liturgy the full and active participation by all the people is the aim to be considered before all else. . . .[23]

A similar concern for participation is evident in Protestant reforms as well, which often refer to the Reformation principle of the "priesthood of all believers" as authority for urging greater congregational participation in the liturgy.[24] Congregational participation in litanies and prayers of intercession reflect this desire, as do preferences for church space arranged in more communal patterns.[25]

There is also, as a result of the liturgical movement in the churches, a fresh awareness of ritual as a basic human activity rather than a mark of neurosis or superstition. Attentiveness to movement and gesture; to space and its arrangement; to the use of elements such as bread, wine, and water, which are capable of bearing the full theological weight placed on them; and to the rhythm of a liturgy is now part of the liturgical renewal process in all traditions and denominations.[26]

COMMON GROUND AND MUTUAL CRITIQUE

Having examined, however briefly, the chief characteristics and values of each movement, we are now in a position to attempt to answer our question about the possibility of finding common ground as well as areas for fruitful dialogue.

Common ground lies, I am persuaded, in three areas: first, the conviction that liturgy is constitutive of a community's identity as well as its faith, and therefore must be the people's work in reality; second, that for a liturgical event to be the people's work in reality it must take seriously the daily lives of those people in social context; third, the conviction that liturgy is more than words and must be embodied in gesture, movement, and attentiveness to physical space. Or, to use terms employed previously, there is common ground in commitment to participation, contextuality (or the pastoral norm), and ritual expressiveness. Underlying these areas of agreement there is more common ground, namely that transforming the church's liturgy is a powerful means of transforming the church's self-understanding and witness to the world. Both movements are convinced that such transformation is both possible and necessary.

There are also areas in which there is some agreement tempered by divergence on particulars. The common concern to moderate the clerically-dominated character of much liturgical practice takes a different form in each movement. The feminist movement has tended to reject authority and roles of authority in favor of communalism or at least some form of group leadership. Ruether has noted that feminist groups engaged in a process of rejecting patriarchal leadership models sometimes go through a stage "in which any talent or expertise is rejected and those who have such talents are sabotaged for exercising leadership."[27] Such a stage is not exclusively negative, however; aside from its value precisely as a "stage" serving a psychological and social purpose for the group, the experience of experimenting with communal or even anarchic models of community is a heady experience for the participants, and perhaps a necessary prerequisite to recognizing legitimate authority and leadership when it arises within a group. As Ruether continues, "once this phase is worked through, it becomes evident that dismantling clerical-ism does not do away with authentic leadership based on function and skills."[28] These are the concerns and processes of a group which has always been denied access to legitimate authority and leadership within the church.

The liturgical movement, being basically a movement led by people who already had access to legitimate authority and leadership, has had different issues with clericalism. Although the liturgical movement would not use terms such as "disman-tling clericalism," the concern to recognize the liturgy as the people's work has shifted the focus from the ordained person to the community. The community is then seen as the "celebrant," the ordained person as the one who "presides" at the community's celebration, by authority of the community and in their service. "The liturgy belongs to no one but the Church, Christ's Body, which is both subject and agent of every liturgical act," observes Aidan Kavanagh. "Since every liturgical act is an ecclesial act, liturgical ministers of whatever order are servants of this act inasmuch as they are servants of the ecclesial assembly."[29] The liturgical movement's concern with clericalism has focused, therefore, on redefining the minister's role as servant to the worshiping community, and has attempted to curtail abuses such as gratuitous concelebrations, the multiplication of unnecessary clergy in roles of leadership, and the clerical usurpation of the people's liturgical actions such as the prayers of the people and the kiss of peace. The use of the image of the servant as a corrective to clericalism is useful only from the perspective of those who already have authority to exercise, and need help in redefining the use of that power.

Feminist liturgical writers rarely use "servant" language to define the exercise of leadership within a group of people who have been culturally and theologically understood as "natural" or divinely appointed servants. Ruether uses the term "ministry of function," referring to such ministers as "helpers" or "enablers" whose basic function is to "equip the community itself to engage in these various activities." Indeed, as she notes, although such ministry may at first be exercised by those who have special competence, as they work as enablers, more and more members of the community will begin to be competent in these specialized ministries, making it possible to rotate the leadership roles and thus "communalize" liturgical leadership.[30]

Yet we should not exaggerate the difference between a "servant" model of leadership and an "enabler" model. The weight of both is on the derivative character of the office which has its source and purpose in the life of the worshipping community. The office in question is radically responsible to the community within which it exists. Servant language emphasizes the responsibility to the community; enabler language recognizes the authority given by the community. Where there is a difference in emphasis, it is due to the social location of the group using the terms.[31]

Although both movements have found a kind of ecumenism in the process of pursuing other goals, the ecumenisms found spring from different sources and accomplish different aims. As already noted, the ecumenism discovered by the liturgical movement grows out of a recovery of a common tradition which predates controversies dividing the present-day churches. Although certainly the ancient church was not free from divisions, the matters which divided the ancient church no longer occupy the attention of contemporary Christians. In spite of these ancient divisions, however, scholars have identified significant areas of consensus on fundamentals such as the shape of the liturgy. This common heritage is now recognized as an important source of ecumenical conversation and celebration.

The feminist liturgical movement, by contrast, lacks a sense of "tradition" because of the critical awareness that the traditioning process has routinely omitted or distorted women and women's roles and contributions. Because women have been excluded from the traditioning process, the movement is suspicious of arguments based on "tradition." Due to this liturgical lacuna, the feminist liturgical movement has had open to it two possible paths: to reject tradition altogether and create liturgies de novo and ad hoc, or to reject patriarchal traditions but reconstruct a feminist religion outside of existing traditions, as the Goddess movement has done. Feminist ecumenism, then, cannot rest on "tradition" as understood by the liturgical movement. Its source must be women's experience, which is more ancient than any religion. By "women's experience," it should be added, a subjective reliance on personal experience is not meant. Rather, "women's experience" is intended to refer to that historical and present reality which has been and continues to be ignored or distorted because of women's enforced silence and lack of access to education and positions of authority. It is collective experience, and it is objectively available to any who wish to study it, as men's experience has always been. Thus the feminist movement's concern with women's experience is neither ahistorical nor antitraditional per se; it is simply concerned with recovering our own history and our own tradition.

Thus it is at the point of the authority of tradition (and, by extension, the Bible) that the feminist movement and the liturgical movement diverge most significantly. Herein lie the areas of possible mutual critique, and thus possible mutual strengthening. Central to this dialogue then will be the issue of tradition: what are its sources, what authority does it carry, and how is it to be used? Or, to put the same question differently, how is tradition constructed? And, what would Christian liturgical tradition look like if it included women's tradition?

The search for an answer to the first question will occupy us in the next chapter; the remaining chapters will explore some aspects of the second. Before turning to those matters, however, it is worth examining the implication that tradition is constructed, and what that might mean for a productive dialogue between these two movements. As observed above, women suffer from amnesia. We lack a sense of tradition, especially where our traditions are concerned, for our association with the liturgy has historically been an association built on limitations. Insofar as we have any sense of liturgical tradition, it is a tradition of restrictions: these things we may not do, these things we may not touch, these places we may not enter, these roles we may not take, these words we may not speak. This negative tradition gives us no sense of participation in the liturgy, no sense that the liturgy is our work. The full, active, and fruitful participation of women in the liturgy demands a construction of tradition in which the lacuna is filled, in which the memory of women is recovered.

All tradition is constructed, for a tradition is not what happened, but what is remembered. Patriarchal tradition remembers what is important for patriarchy to remember, what is important for its survival and for its identity. Feminist tradition likewise must be constructed partly in order to correct and strengthen the partial vision of the church's present tradition, but also to assist women in our struggle for survival and identity. Post-Christian and post-Jewish feminists have begun already to do such constructive work, taking fragments of ancient prehistory and common experiences of women's oppression to construct a tradition which evokes a time when women "were not slaves."[32] This constructive remembering is available to feminists in biblical religion as well.

Elisabeth Schüssler Fiorenza has identified a process of feminist interpretation of the Bible which recognizes the possibilities of and necessity for such a construction. She identifies four stages in this process, which she names hermeneutics of suspicion, hermeneutics of proclamation, hermeneutics of remembrance, and hermeneutics of creative actualization. A hermeneutics of suspicion recognizes the androcentric and patriarchal character of the biblical text, as the feminist liturgical movement recognizes the androcentric and patriarchal character of the liturgical tradition. A hermeneutics of proclamation recognizes that the Bible is still a part of a living tradition, not only a historical document, and recognizes women's participation in that tradition. A hermeneutics of remembrance "moves history." And a hermeneutics of creative actualization extends the remembrance of women's biblical history into the present by means of creative participation in the continuation of the biblical story of liberation.[33]

The result of this process is the construction of a biblical tradition that includes rather than excludes women, not only in the text, but also in the process of interpretation. A similar process can serve for the construction of feminist liturgical tradition. The liturgical tradition, like the biblical tradition, is both androcentric and patriarchal. That is to say, it takes male perspective as the normative human perspective, and reinforces male authority at the expense of women and low-status males. However, unlike the Bible, the liturgical tradition is not based on a text (although there are, of course, liturgical texts) but on a repeated event, the liturgical event. This opens up the realms of the non-verbal and visual as well as the verbal. Moreover, since the liturgy precedes the canonization of the books of the Bible, and even the writing of them (or grew at the same time as the writing of them), then it is possible that the liturgical tradition contains the evidence (albeit distorted or hidden) of a non-patriarchal Christian tradition of the sort that Schüssler Fiorenza identifies in the New Testament.

Although a method derived from feminist biblical hermeneutics could be developed for the interpretation of liturgical texts, what concerns us here is the interpretation of liturgical events. Thus we are interested in the process of constructing a tradition in its general outlines. For our purposes, then, we note the emphasis throughout on remembering (tradition) and imagination (creative actualization). The reconstruction of women's history depends on the remembering of women; creative actualization in liturgical celebration depends on the reconstructed remembrance of women.

So it is in liturgical reconstruction. The construction of a feminist liturgical tradition demands that women's experience be remembered and respected, not as marginal to the tradition, but as a necessary part of it. The remembrance of women's experience requires imagination, because so much has been lost, forgotten, and distorted.

CHAPTER TWO

SOMETHING MISSING

Memory and Imagination

Constructing feminist liturgical tradition requires two things: a feminist reconstruction of our common liturgical memory, and a feminist enlargement of our common liturgical imagination.

It may appear at first glance that memory and imagination are opposing concepts. Memory, after all, is concerned with the past—an interpreted past, certainly, but real events in any case. Imagination, as the term is commonly used, suggests flights of fancy unfettered by anything so mundane as historical events. Indeed, imagination is sometimes used as a way to escape from painful memories or rejected past. However, as this chapter will argue, the two concepts are in fact deeply related to one another, and are equally essential to the full and authentic celebration of Christian liturgy.

Contemporary women in biblical religions suffer from liturgical amnesia, a lack of a liturgical tradition that remembers, celebrates, and mourns the memory of women. By "the memory of women," I mean the memory of particular women, and the memories that women have preserved. Countless names, stories, and experiences of women who have gone before us in the faith have been forgotten. Without them as part of our living memory and of our liturgical memorials, we have no measure against which to judge who we are or who we might be.

This is a very grave matter for women in a religion with anamnesis at its heart, as Christianity is. It is a grave matter for Christianity as well. All of Christian liturgy requires a profound remembering, which renews and reclaims the significance of past events for the present. Without this firm grounding in the particularity of historical events, which make liturgical celebration possible when connected with God's faithfulness, Christianity runs the risk of drifting off into gnosticism. But Christian liturgy also suffers when its memory of those particulars is faulty or incomplete. Then Christian liturgy may tend toward heresy or self-deception.[1] Thus the restoration of women's memory to liturgical anamnesis is of critical importance to the church as a whole, as well as to women whose memories have been distorted, misused, or ignored.

We also suffer from restricted imaginations. Our imaginations as women have been "colonized" by patriarchal culture, a process Adrienne Rich calls "arts of survival turned to rituals of self-hatred."[2] Anamnesis for women requires the creation of feminist imagination, which permits women to appropriate our past and to envision our future in ways that reject self-hatred and make survival possible. As we shall explore shortly, the reconstruction of women's liturgical tradition demands the use of "historical imagination," or what Elisabeth Schüssler Fiorenza also calls "hermeneutics of remembrance." The silencing of women past and present makes necessary an imaginative process of identifying with the invisible and silent women of the tradition, to make them both visible and audible.

But the need for feminist imagination goes beyond its usefulness to historical reconstruction. Imagination has a constructive purpose as well as a reconstructive one. As the word itself suggests, imagination is a way of seeing. In a patriarchal culture, androcentric and patriarchal seeing are normative for everyone, men and women alike, and patriarchal and androcentric seeing views women as deviant from the male norm and as subservient to patriarchal authority. The effect of this on women is a devaluation of the self and of all other women which amounts to the kind of self-hatred Rich speaks of. The development of feminist imagination, however, is simultaneously critical of patriarchal seeing and engaged in creating new ways of seeing.

A feminist imagination is concerned with two kinds of seeing, both of which might well be called prophetic. The first kind of feminist seeing is concerned with the present, and strives to transcend the limits of patriarchal reality by continually asking: is it true for us? The second kind of feminist seeing allows us to participate in the construction of the future. If a failed or suppressed imagination produces cramped and lifeless visions of the future, a freed imagination can generate expansive and lifegiving visions. The operation of the imagination enables us to leap past the limits of what is and what has been to what might be.

Because Christian liturgy is at a fundamental level an action of the imagination, this too is a serious theological matter. Insofar as the liturgical tradition has been shaped by patriarchal imagination, its ability both to appropriate events of the past and to generate compelling and freeing visions of the future is suppressed. However, even more particularly, the use of the imagination is essential for the celebration of the sacraments and for the development of a sacramental understanding of all of life. We will explore in depth the significance of the creation of feminist liturgical anamnesis and feminist liturgical imagination for the central Christian sacraments of baptism and eucharist in a later chapter. But first we must concern ourselves with making plain what we mean by "feminist liturgical anamnesis" and "feminist liturgical imagination."

LITURGICAL ANAMNESIS AND WOMEN'S MEMORY

At the beginning of the passion narratives of both Matthew and Mark, Jesus receives a Messianic anointing with precious oil by a woman disciple (Matt. 26:6-13; Mark 14:3-9). Over the protests of the male disciples, Jesus praises the woman's act, and promises that it will be told in her memory wherever the gospel is proclaimed. However, by the time the gospels were written down, the woman's name had already been forgotten.[3] It is important to note that the context and the content of the story are thoroughly liturgical—she performs a significant and readily recognizable liturgical act, that of anointing. And Jesus' promise to her is a liturgical one, involving proclamation and remembering. Yet there is no trace of the woman and her liturgical action in our liturgical commemorations of the passion of Jesus. Our lectionaries largely ignore her,[4] our liturgies of anointing do not remember her, our sanctoral cycles confuse her with Mary of Bethany or Mary Magdalene.[5] The church has not kept Jesus' promise to this woman.

The story of the forgotten woman and her liturgical act stands as a paradigm of the failure of the church in its liturgy not only to remember women and their liturgical-prophetic deeds, but also to respect women's memories. For the church not only failed to remember the woman's name; it also failed to remember the significance of the event, as, for example, Luke's redaction of the story shows.[6] It also shows that the forgetting and distorting have not been accidental or innocent, but quite intentional and selective. The church indeed cannot be said to have forgotten women; it has remembered women when we have seemed to be troublesome or dangerous, and when we have been docile or useful. But it has forgotten to take women and our memories seriously, even when commanded by Jesus to do so.

Before we turn to a consideration of the liturgical significance of anamnesis and its feminist reconstruction, it should be noted that the proposal to include women's memory in liturgical anamnesis is not simply a matter of adding a few women's names to the eucharistic text or increasing the number of lectionary texts which mention women. Rather, the locating of women's memory in Christian liturgical anamnesis will yield a profound reexperiencing of the entire Christian tradition.

ANAMNESIS AND MEMORY

Remembering is a fundamentally human act. Humans remember both spontaneously and intentionally. Our remembering is purposeful and meaningful. From our memories we construct our identity, interpret the significance of experiences (both our own and others'), and live in relationship with others. Our memory of the past and our sense of living in continuity with it makes possible both faithfulness and judgment.[7] Artist Judy Chicago says, speaking of the recovery of women's history, "Our history is our power." But even more powerful than our history is our memory, which is our personalized and internalized history. A person with amnesia lacks personal identity because of loss of memory; and the loss of memory, of known past, ironically locks one into the past, in a search for that which is missing.

What is true of individuals and their need for memory is also true for communities and groups. The effect of the recovery of "lost histories" of women, black Americans, and Native Americans has been a recovery of a sense of power and identity within those groups and renewed hope for the future. The lack of a collective memory, or tradition, damages or destroys the identity of a group and places the members of that group at the mercy of others, who would define the group for their own advantage. As in the case of an individual with amnesia, the loss of memory prevents a group or community from living fully in the present or looking forward to the future. Groups such as women, black Americans, and Native Americans have been subject to oppression in large part because they have been denied their history.

The use of the term "lost history" here and elsewhere must not be taken to suggest that oppressed groups are responsible for the "loss" of their history. In fact, history-making and tradition-keeping have not been in the hands of oppressed people. Thus their stories and memories, although in some cases remembered by the oppressed community, are "forgotten" by the official history-keepers. Indeed, the suppression of such stories and memories is an essential element in sustaining oppression. This suppression, which sometimes takes the form of distortion or misuse of history, generates "lost history." This distorted and partial history, which claims to be true and complete, produces amnesia among those whose stories have been lost.

For Christians as a group, a sense of collective memory is basic to identity. To the individual Christian, identity and meaning, faithfulness and judgment, and life lived in relationship are all influenced more or less profoundly by the recollection of the Christian past and by the development of a Christian memory. Likewise, Christian communities depend on a sense of continuity with the whole of salvation history, as well as the place of particular Christian events within it. Indeed, the significance of particular Christian events is given deeper meaning and greater power by virtue of being interpreted within the larger history of salvation.

Because to remember one's past is to have a future, Christian liturgy, which recalls past constitutive events, inevitably is oriented toward an eschatological future.[8] The Christian eschatological hope is firmly grounded in the memory and the faithfulness of God, and thus in the conviction that God will not forget us.

The term *anamnesis* has its locus in liturgical action. Liturgical anamnesis involves not only remembering with the mind but also remembering with the body (individual and collective). More than the repetition of words, liturgical anamnesis involves the use of the body in gesture and movement.[9] This characteristic reminds us of divine activity embodied in history, the Word made flesh. It also brings, experientially and dramatically, divine activity into the present, not only in time but in space. The human body and human community then are seen as the locus for this activity.

This embodied remembering is found at the center of all Christian liturgy insofar as that liturgy remembers, and remembering, celebrates the Paschal Mystery of Jesus Christ crucified, dead, risen, and present in the power of the Spirit. It is found generously extended and elaborated in the church year.[10] It appears condensed and terse in the anaphora. It is recognized and hymned in rising sun and evening light in the daily office.[11]

Studies of the Christian use of *anamnesis* have been illuminated by an exploration of the significance of the Hebrew parallels which lie behind it. The Hebrew concept of "memorial" or "remembrance" has several characteristics also found (to greater or lesser degree) in Christian liturgy.[12] Its primary context and usage in Hebrew scripture is cultic, especially in reference to feasts, offerings, and cultic objects. This "remembrance" is not a purely mental exercise, but concrete action, involving events, people, and objects.[13] It is commonly associated with the powerful concept of the "name." Remembering is equivalent to naming, and to remember God's name is to acknowledge one's relationship with God. Similarly, to be remembered by God is to be assured of God's tender concern: Yahweh "remembered" Rachel (Gen. 30:22) and Hannah (I Sam. 1:11, 19-20) and answered their prayers for children.[14] God remembers not only individuals, but also God's own covenants (Gen. 9:16, 19:29; Lev. 26:42-43; Deut. 9:27; Ezek. 16:60-63; Pss. 104:8-10, 105:45, 110:4-5, etc.), and remembering, again shows divine favor and mercy. The people, too, remember God's covenants, especially in their memorial feasts. The remembrance of God's gracious acts evokes in the rememberer acts of thanksgiving and praise toward God and righteousness and mercy toward people (Exod. 12:14-15; Deut. 7:18, 15:15; Jonah 2:8, 10, etc.).[15] Manifestly, the notion of remembrance found in Hebrew scriptures is dialogical, effective, and concrete (or embodied). It is dialogical because it presumes a relationship between God and people; effective, because the remembering calls forth a response, whether from God or from people; concrete because it involves specifics such as names, people, actions, and objects.

To a certain extent, these characteristics have also carried over into Christian liturgy. The remembrance of the divine name becomes associated with the name of Jesus, by whose authority Christian prayer is offered and cultic acts performed.[16] Later this association is expanded to the name of the Trinity. Names of individuals are remembered in the intercessions before the anaphora or in the diptychs of the anaphora itself,[17] in the intercessions of the cathedral office, in the baptismal rite, and in the sanctoral cycle. In both remembrance of the divine name and remembrance of individuals, response in the form of action is expected.

More narrowly, anamnesis is located at the heart of the constitutive Christian rite, the Eucharistic prayer. It is found in all of the most ancient anaphoras where it connects the proclamation of the past constitutive event, the institution narrative, with the present action of offering of bread and wine as memorial sacrifice. It makes possible the petition for the Holy Spirit and intercessions for the saints of the church which follow.[18]

But of course anamnesis is not limited to these few lines; it occurs not only in the immediate context of the institution narrative, but also in the broader context of the thanksgiving, which remembers not only the events of the Last Supper but also the broader sweep of God's mighty acts. The creedal character of the eucharistic prayer has been noted, and Dom Botte has drawn attention to the creedal character of the expansions of the anamnesis to include other mysteries of Christ in addition to the death and resurrection.[19] This may well be interpreted as a case of dogma influencing the liturgy. But it also may be interpreted in the light of the foregoing discussion of the name as a form of anamnesis. Particularly in the instance of the *berakah*, the identity of the God who is addressed is made clear by a statement of God's actions.[20] The remembering of the mysteries of Christ—conception, nativity, baptism, death, burial, resurrection, ascension—becomes a way of naming God by enumerating God's mighty acts in Jesus Christ. The naming and remembering are made more concrete by being more particular.

The action-orientation is also seen in the Eucharistic anamnesis, which itself is the action ("remembering"-"offering") commanded by Christ at the conclusion of the narrative: "Do this." Also in common with the concept of memorial found in Hebrew scriptures is the remembering of the covenant with God; in the case of Christian liturgy, of course, it is not only the covenants with the Jewish Patriarchs which are recalled, but primarily the new covenant in Jesus Christ. And in both Hebrew and Christian usage, the purpose of this process of naming-remembering-acting is to generate an encounter with God which is both personal and collective, and which introduces one into a new reality.[21]

The discussion of Christian anamnesis thus far has focused, as has the Western Christian tradition generally, on anamnesis as "reminding people." But as we have seen, "reminding-God" was and is a significant aspect of memorial in Jewish liturgical tradition. For oppressed people, however, and any who have felt abandoned by God, the "reminding-God" aspect is critically important. For profound suffering, loss of identity, and inability to anticipate the future call into question the beneficence or at least the omnipotence of God.[22] The reminding of God also recognizes a fundamental truth: to be forgotten by God is to die; to be remembered by God is to live.

This sense of abandonment by God, coming from experiences of suffering, is for women intensified by the liturgy's forgetfulness. The liturgy has preserved and ritualized patriarchal memory. As in the case of biblical texts, the memories of women or about women which survive come through the lens of patriarchal memory. Although the name God gives Moses is circumspect enough about God's gender, the titles given to that God are patriarchal: Lord, King, husband, father. Although the classical Roman rite preferred qualities or actions of God to titles ("Almighty and merciful God," "God who . . . ,") contemporary translations have emphasized the title "Father."[23] Trinitarian language developed in a patriarchal context and accepted androcentric norms, as did the liturgy.[24] God is addressed and referred to in the liturgy as male.

The remembrance of constitutive events in salvation-history is likewise androcentric. The commandments were given to and addressed to men ("you shall not covet your neighbor's wife . . ."), and the covenants were made with men.[25] Women are remembered only tangentially through relationships with men. Feminist biblical scholars have shown how active women were in Judaism, in the ministry of Jesus, and in the early Church; they have also demonstrated how often women have been forgotten, ignored, discounted, and reinterpreted in the tradition. The events and people memorialized in scripture, tradition, and liturgy reflect an androcentric bias. This is seen in the organization of our contemporary lectionaries, which omit texts about Deborah, Judith, Rachel and Leah, Tabitha, Lydia, Priscilla, and the daughters of Philip, and which include women on the basis of their association with male heroes and actors.[26] It is also reflected in the sanctoral cycle, in which male clerics overwhelmingly outnumber women saints.[27] When women are memorialized, their memory is distorted or reinterpreted to fit patriarchal categories. Thus the image of Mary Magdalene, first witness to the resurrection, is distorted because the Western liturgical tradition identifies her as a prostitute. The anonymous woman who anoints Jesus before his death is forgotten or confused with women in other stories. Even the memory of powerful Goddess figures preserved in devotion to Mary and to some female saints is turned to patriarchal use.[28]

This progressive loss of women's heritage and memory in the loss or distorting of names has had profound consequences for women. As we have seen, the Hebrew tradition identified the forgetting of names as the equivalent of death for the ones forgotten. Our past as women in biblical religion has been allowed to die because our memorial has not been kept in a patriarchal and androcentric tradition. The names of our foremothers, their deeds, and their encounters with the divine have been forgotten.

But we have lost more than our history, as serious as this is. Liturgical anamnesis, I have argued, is more than mental remembering; it is *embodied* remembering, and as such involves action and the use of the body in a way which communicates the sacredness of that body as locus of divine activity. This too has been lost for women through the gradual restriction of ritual acts to men and the barring of women from sacred spaces, and through the devaluing of women's bodies as dangerous, weak, and polluting.

WOMEN'S MEMORY

The feminist work to be considered here may be viewed as falling into two categories: historical recovery and imaginative work. The work of recovering women's past has been characterized by critical interpretation of history in light of the present and with a sense of responsibility toward the future, our own and our daughters'. This process of recovery has prompted a reassessment and reinterpretation of both accustomed historical assumptions, and religious structures and traditions.[29] It has revealed women as victims of those traditions and of religions' official traditioning processes. It has also shown the ways in which women have struggled, adapted, and survived in patriarchal institutions in spite of opposition and oppression. The purpose of this historical recovery has been the reconstruction of women's memory.

In imaginative works of fiction, poetry, and art, women's memories are not only brought to light, but given life. True to the earlier observation about the past enabling the future, many times these works are able not only to evoke women's memories, but also to imagine the possibilities for the future. Since liturgical anamnesis requires both memory of the past and the imaginative bridge from past to present and future, both of these categories of feminist work are necessary to the recovery of women's liturgical anamnesis.

Among feminist biblical scholars engaged in the recovery of women's memory Elisabeth Schüssler Fiorenza in New Testament and Phyllis Trible in Old Testament have had the most influence. Although employing different methodologies, both set out to recover women's past in order to put it at the service of present-day and future women in biblical religions.

Phyllis Trible's major works, *God and the Rhetoric of Sexuality*[30] and *Texts of Terror*[31], seek to recover and reinterpret Scripture texts about women. In the first book, the search is for treasures lost, as the woman searches for her lost coin (Luke 15:8-10), and, like the woman of the parable, there is rejoicing in the finding. What is recovered is not only valuable for women, but positive as well. Hidden beneath and within patriarchal texts are found texts which affirm the dignity, value, and sacredness of women's lives and bodies. The search in *Texts of Terror* is different. It looks for not only the forgotten texts about women, but also texts that show the suffering of women, often as forgotten and neglected as texts that celebrate women. This book "recounts tales of terror *in memoriam* . . . in order to recover a neglected history, to remember a past that the present embodies, and to pray that these terrors shall not come to pass again."[32] Taken together, Trible's two works are an important reminder that the recovery of women's memory is not painless. It involves not only celebration of valor, beauty, and survival, but also a lament for loss, abandonment, and terror. It also forces us to recognize the continuity between past and present. Women are still victims of betrayal, rape, and violence, and women still struggle courageously and survive with dignity against terrible odds. Liturgically, acts of both thanksgiving and lament are called for.[33]

In the field of New Testament studies Elisabeth Schüssler Fiorenza's magisterial *In Memory of Her,* as its title implies, painstakingly reconstructs the early history of Christianity by restoring women to the center of that history. Her work is intended to help Christian feminists "reclaim their suffering and struggles in and through the subversive power of the 'remembered past.' Such a 'subversive memory' not only keeps alive the suffering and hopes of Christian women in the past but also allows for a universal solidarity of sisterhood with all women of the past, present, and future who follow the same vision."[34] This "subversive memory," which Schüssler Fiorenza has restored to us unflinchingly identifies the androcentric mindset and patriarchal context of the New Testament writings, and displays the consequences of those facts for the freedom, power, and identity of early Christian women. At the same time this memory also includes women in early Christianity who were confident in their freedom, power, and identity, and who were far from being either marginal or submissive. In the struggle of women to maintain their identity and to exercise their freedom in the face of patriarchal suppression and forgetfulness, Schüssler Fiorenza finds the common bond that unites women across religious and cultural barriers, "subversive memory." It should be added that it also unites women across barriers of time, since contemporary women are still engaged in the same struggle.

The spiritual consequences of this restored memory are not

backward-looking but forward-looking. Schüssler Fiorenza proposes understanding the New Testament as prototype, not as an archetype which identifies changeless truths with patriarchal texts. Rather than seeking to return to a "golden age," this model makes transformation possible, and projection into the future inescapable.[35] The memory creates a "vision" of early Christian women, which "must be allowed to become a transformative power that can open up a feminist future for women in biblical religion."[36] The result is an "*ekklesia* of women," the identification of women as church.

The image of *ekklesia* of women places women firmly at the center of the Christian tradition and legitimates the gathering of women to celebrate their faith, while rejecting images that would claim spiritual superiority for women or demand separatism from the church. This *ekklesia* of women, born of the memory of the struggle of Christian women, is communal, active in soldarity with the oppressed, and embodied.

> Bodily existence is not detrimental or peripheral to our spiritual becoming as the *ekklesia* of women but constitutive and central to it. . . . How can we point to the eucharistic bread and say "this is my body" as long as women's bodies are battered, raped, sterilized, mutilated, prostituted, and used to male ends? . . . Therefore, the *ekklesia* of women must reclaim women's bodies as the "image and body of Christ. . . ."[37]

This emphasis on embodiment is particularly important, since women's bodies have been and continue to be devalued and abused. To claim that "women's bodies are the body of Christ" is to claim women's bodies as sacred and the abuse of women's bodies as sacrilege. It also grounds the *ekklesia* of women firmly in the physical world and demands liturgical expression which is likewise embodied.

Liturgically, the "subversive memory" recovered by Schüssler Fiorenza's work calls forth "creative actualization": the generation of new liturgies, hymns, and stories of women which reconstruct the past and shape the future.[38] This is nothing less than a call to allow the historical reconstructions of our past as women of biblical religions to become part of our collective memory. This exercise in historical imagination[39] is a means of connecting women in the present with women of the past: transforming history into anamnesis for women.

Such imaginative appropriation of feminist history, whether Trible's literary imagination or Schüssler Fiorenza's historical imagination, is an essential ingredient in the reconstruction of women's memory and the development of feminist anamnesis. For this process, works of feminist artists, poets, and novelists are essential resources. The works of artists such as Judy Chicago and Meinrad Craighead offer new images of women and of God which challenge our existing patriarchal images and are created out of a sense of the sacredness of women's bodies and women's experiences.[40] Poets such as Marge Piercy, Judy Grahn, Adrienne Rich, Ntozake Shange, and Alice Walker have dared to speak the truth about the particularity of women's lives and hopes.[41] In her poetry, Adrienne Rich employs a rich variety of images to describe women in the process of searching for their past and reconstructing their lives: a diver "diving into the wreck," searching for "the wreck and not the story of the wreck, the thing itself and not the myth"; miners "stooping to half our height to bring the essential vein to light"; the spider with "the passion to make and make again where such unmaking reigns, the refusal to be a victim"; the woman piecing together a work of patchwork, "dark against light, silk against roughness, pulling the tenets of a life together."[42] In every case grief and anger over all that has been lost, destroyed, and forgotten fuels the determination "to make and make again." Rich often uses the term "remember," sometimes writing it "re-member" to emphasize the bodiliness of the act of remembering, as when a woman is "rehearsing in her body . . . a tale only she can tell."[43]

This particularity of women's memory and experience influences also the work of writers Ntozake Shange and Alice Walker, who undertake to recover the most hidden and most "dangerous" memories of our culture, those of women of color. The complex and painful interweaving of oppression based on race and sex are unflinchingly exposed, and the courage and beauty of black women are celebrated. Shange's choreopoem *For Colored Girls* speaks of "missin somethin," "a layin on of hands"; Walker's Celie in *The Color Purple* struggles against a God who is "an old white man" who has never done any good for her. Out of this consciousness of loss and of absence, they discover the holiness of themselves—"I found God in myself and I loved her fiercely"—and in their connectedness with nature—"If I cut a tree, I bleed."[44] The memory of black American women is marked by the particularities of their struggles against slavery, racism, and sexism and by the need for liberation and self-love. Walker's definition of "womanist" sums this up: "Loves music. Loves dance. Loves the moon. *Loves* the Spirit. Loves love and food and roundness. Loves struggle. *Loves* the Folk. Loves herself. *Regardless.*"[45]

This construction of a new spirituality out of the memory of women's struggles and hopes has called forth literature able imaginatively to reconstruct a history in which women kept their own traditions alive. In Anne Cameron's *Daughters of Copper Woman,* the stories of the Nootka people of Vancouver Island are kept and retold by the members of the secret Women's Society. They remember the origins of their tribe in Copper Woman, who becomes Old Woman, who becomes "part of all creation." They remember a time when women and men lived together in peace and freedom. They also remember the invasion of Western explorers and the coming of Christianity, which brought disease, rape, self-hatred, and the destruction of their culture. The memory passed on by the Women's Society is not only mythic but also living memory, remembering a time when women loved their own bodies, were respected and valued. The importance of the memories, however, is not backward-looking but forward-looking. As Cameron says in the preface, "There is a better way of doing things. Some of us remember that better way."[46] As in the other examples cited, the loss of the past is mourned: "Who cannot love herSelf cannot love anybody;" but the ultimate hope is the recovery of the sense of the self as powerful and beautiful: "I have been searching Old Woman and I find her in mySelf."[47] Essential to this recovery, however, is the recognition of the particular, and therefore partial, nature of what is remembered: "Scattered pieces from the black sisters, from the yellow sisters, from the white sisters, are coming together, trying to form a whole, and it can't form without the pieces we have saved and cherished."[48] Implicit in the stories of *Daughters of Copper Woman* is the challenge to all women to claim their memory, tradition, stories, in all their particularity, as a way to recovering the vision of the whole.

This recovery of particularity is found also in Kim Chernin's novel, *The Flame Bearers*. Living in contemporary San Francisco, the women of the novel are members of an Orthodox Jewish family in which traditional patriarchal Judaism is practiced alongside an ancient women's tradition of Goddess-worship. The tradition is kept alive by the women, who pass on the lore and rituals from mother to daughter. The memory and practice of this worship is not perceived as over against traditional Judaism, but is seen as an essential part of it which has been forgotten and suppressed, but eventually must once again come to light. This process of forgetting and remembering is explained by one of the women characters, Naamah the scribe: "This is what happens. When the people as a whole forget, the women remember. They keep the secret, now that it has become a secret. They tell it as stories, from mother to daughter. It is the same all over the world."[49] As in the case of the secret character of the Women's Society described in *Copper Woman*, the secrecy is not native to women's memory, but a necessity imposed on women by oppression. The knowledge and memory is forced to go underground in order to preserve it for the future, for some time when it will no longer be necessary for it to be kept secret, when it will be needed. The decision to reclaim the forgotten and suppressed memory may be motivated partly out of a sense that the knowledge will be accepted, and partly out of a sense of the extremity of need. Whether lost or secret, women's memory is now being recovered both because recent social movements have encouraged it and also because the instinct for survival—not only of women but also of the planet—seems to demand it.[50]

WOMEN'S LITURGICAL ANAMNESIS

That a time of crisis and possibility is upon us is reflected in the publication of works such as those cited above. It may also be seen in the evolution of worshiping communities of women, both within biblical religions and outside them. Some of these Christian communities are described in Rosemary Radford Ruether's *Women-Church: Theology and Practice.*[51] Within such communities women's memory is preserved and celebrated in liturgical act and word.

This liturgical *anamnesis* of women is characteristically feminist. That is, it is simultaneously critical of existing patriarchal traditions and texts and committed to the principle that women's memory and experience is both legitimate and central to our religious traditions. It takes with utmost seriousness the need to remember the names of women before the community and before God. The memorializing of women from the past reminds us of our responsibility to them and to the continuation of our common work in the future. Such remembering, as we have seen, is often painful and terrible. The active remembering of the sufferings and struggles and hopes of the past will demand lament as often as thanksgiving. Acknowledgment that we are "missin somethin" must precede the search for it. Lament over that which has been lost and rejection (or exorcism) of that which is destructive also must precede reconciliation, healing, and celebration.

Feminist liturgical anamnesis also remembers the name of God as many names, especially as female names. Naming God as female and as varied makes it possible to affirm particularity in encounters between people and the Holy One. Naming God as female also affirms the value and sacredness of women who are varied: Ntozake Shange and the Nootka woman can both find God "in mySelf." If the Holy One can be named female, then female bodies and experiences can be holy.

Memories and experiences of the female body and its rhythms are no longer either marginal or negative, but central to a more complete understanding of God, self, and community. Rituals for first menstruation, monthly menstruation, birth, and menopause are being developed and used by women in biblical religions.[52] Because women's bodies have also been objects of abuse, rituals of healing are also needed for victims of incest, violence, and rape.[53] The Christian tradition that "your body is a temple of the Holy Spirit" (I Cor. 6:19) must be reclaimed for women in particular so that we too may "glorify God in our bodies."

To put it as simply as possible, feminist liturgical anamnesis is the active remembrance of our collective past as seen through women's eyes and experienced in women's bodies. This is necessary not to fragment further the Christian community, but to restore to it that which has been missing from it. Only by recognizing the particularity of such remembering are reconciliation and wholeness possible.

The method for this process is twofold: a process of reclamation and reconstruction. A process of reclamation must return to our traditional liturgical texts, as we have returned to biblical texts, in order to identify the oppressive and the liberating strata. Liturgical texts must be subjected to critical scrutiny so that distortions, omissions, and misuses of women's memory and experience can be identified. Texts must also be mined for surviving fragments of the memory of women's experience, on the assumption that women have always been part of the church and thus must have left some mark on their worship.[54]

The process of reconstruction demands the use of the imagination. From Schüssler Fiorenza's historical imagination we must move to liturgical imagination. Such a process is hardly foreign to the liturgy. *Anamnesis* is not *mimesis*. Eucharistic texts do not always limit themselves to direct biblical quotation of the institution narrative, but conflate and elaborate on the memory recalled therein.[55] The evolution of the church year shows little or no interest, in its early stages, in historical reconstruction; it is instead based on religious experience and theological conviction.[56] Both the Christian scriptures and the Christian liturgy display an imaginative appropriation of events, persons, and texts from Hebrew scripture, newly interpreted and placed in a new context. By its nature, the liturgy is interpretive and imaginative, since it directs our attention to a reality which goes beyond everyday reality. This process must now be employed in the service of a feminist reconstruction of our common liturgical memory.

IMAGINATION AND *MYSTERION*

If the theological and liturgical significance of memory is manifest, the importance of imagination is perhaps less so. Western theological reflection has been influenced more by discursive and logical thought than by imaginative methods or by attention to drama, story, music, or art.[57] Yet the liturgy has more in common with such imaginative enterprises as drama, story, music, and art than with linear, rational discourse. Indeed, the use of the methods of rationalism have generally not served liturgical theology well, since they fail to take into account liturgy's profoundly nonrational character. Only by understanding liturgy as a deeply imaginative act can we account for liturgy's claim that a bowl of water is the Red Sea, the cosmic waters of chaos, the River Jordan, the uterine waters of new birth, or that a loaf of bread and a cup of wine are the body and blood of the Risen Christ, the foretaste of the messianic banquet, the food of angels. Our ability to perceive these realities is often named "faith," but faith has also come to mean adherence to certain prescribed rational doctrines rationally apprehended. By using the term "imagination" to describe our participation in the reality presented in the liturgy, we are free to move beyond the discursive mode.

This imaginative dimension of the liturgy is often referred to as "mystery," or by use of its Greek equivalent *mysterion*. Although the basic meaning of the Greek *mysterion* is "something on which silence must be kept," in Christian usage it came to mean that which God has revealed to humanity through Jesus Christ.[58] Although in particular New Testament texts the term has different objects—the "mystery of the Kingdom," the "mystery of Christ," the "mystery of the

Church"—its general meaning is that of revelation, especially God's self-revelation.[59]

The church came to recognize that God was significantly revealed in the events of baptism and eucharist. Because the Latin term used to translate *mysterion* was *sacramentum,* we have come to call these and other significant occasions of God's self-disclosure "sacraments." But as James White notes, *mysterion* is perhaps a better term for these occasions because of its suggestions of revelation.[60] At the same time, the English word "mystery" is not satisfactory, since its common-usage meaning implies something hidden or obscure. I would argue that the idea of imagination is helpful for grasping this revelatory aspect of liturgy and the sacraments because of its suggestion of vision, in this case, God-given vision. The significance of imagination for feminist appropriation of the sacraments of baptism and eucharist is explored in chapter 6. What interests us here is drawing out the implications of imagination as a norm for liturgy in general and for the construction of feminist liturgy in particular.

Imagination, or as some express it, theopoetic, implies several things important for the liturgy. It makes possible a sense of paradox and multivalence which is necessary for authentic liturgical celebration; that is to say, it makes symbols possible. It keeps liturgical forms and symbols flexible; that is, it allows liturgy to be the work of the Spirit. And it brings together the verbal, the physical, and the emotional life of worshipers in a common vision; that is, it makes community possible.

FEMINIST IMAGINATION

Within feminist theory, imagination plays a significant role, as we have already examined in part in relation to the reconstruction of feminist memory. But it plays as important a role in the sustaining of a feminist vision of the future. Speaking of poetry as imaginative literature, poet Audre Lorde says:

> For women, then, poetry is not a luxury. It is a vital necessity of our existence. It forms the quality of the light within which we predicate our hopes and dreams toward survival and change, first made into language, then into idea, then into more tangible action. Poetry is the way we help give names to the nameless so it can be thought.[61]

The imaginative enterprise, then, whether it be poetry or some other such activity, is necessary to women's existence, as the locus of our generation of possibilities for the future. It is necessary because the past and the present offer so little evidence of hope, such limited possibilities for survival and change.

FEMINIST LITURGICAL IMAGINATION

For women in biblical religion, the bringing together of our feminist imagination and our liturgical imagination is necessary for our spiritual survival. Essential to this process are not only biblical interpreters who give presence and voice to women from our biblical heritage and historians who do the same for women of our more recent past, but also poets and artists who "form the quality of the light" by which we begin to see the future into which we wish to move, into which the Spirit moves us. The interpretive and imaginative nature of the liturgy can be opened up and transformed by the use of feminist liturgical imagination, which takes seriously women's experience and recognizes its legitimacy as religious experience. For if *mysterion* is the evidence of God's self-revelation to God's people, what of God's self has been revealed to women in biblical religion? Resources for the answer to this question must be sought in scriptural text and historical story, in anamnesis. But if God continues to reveal God's self to people, then we must look as well to contemporary experiences of women. The evidence of contemporary feminist creative work in liturgy, poetry, art, and story suggests some significant common places of God's self-disclosure to women.

We have observed some of the places in the context of our discussion of feminist anamnesis, but they may be recalled here. God is perceived as present in and working through women's struggle for survival and dignity; in the particularity of women's experience which recognizes differences of race, class, age, culture; in experiences of embodiment, especially experiences coming from having women's bodies; in experiences of connectedness with all of creation; in the "tiny acts of immense courage" which are women's daily work; and in experiences of love of self as woman and of other women. Far from identifying with traditional church-centered loci of revelation, this feminist *mysterion* claims hieratic status for these experiences of women, and claims that through them God chooses to reveal God's self. In this instance, the usual meaning of "mystery" serves well, for these aspects of women's lives have been obscure and silence about them has been imposed. But in the Christian adaptation of the term, we may also say that they are now being revealed.

By way of example, let us return to the gospel story discussed earlier in this chapter, the story of the woman who anoints Jesus before his death. Historical reconstruction of that story recognizes that the woman's act was a "prophetic sign-action," identifying Jesus as the Anointed One.[62] Within the Jewish tradition, this was a liturgical act performed by prophets as a way of making kings, and it was also so used in the Western medieval tradition. Within the gospel tradition, it is also a political act, challenging to both religious and political power structures.[63]

Liturgical reconstruction of the story sees in the anointing a baptismal motif: the anointing with oil as expression of the Messianic royal priesthood into which the initiate is introduced is a significant act in ancient baptismal rites.[64] As the baptism of Jesus in the Jordan by John became a prototype of Christian baptism, which emphasized divine election in the gift of the Holy Spirit, so this story can become a prototype of baptismal anointing, emphasizing the Messianic, priestly gifts of baptism. The story's location in the Gospels at the beginning of the Passion narrative also links baptism with Jesus' suffering and death, a connection which was already made by Paul (Rom. 6:3-4). But it also expresses the political implications of baptism, as a challenge to existing oppressive structures and the foundation of an alternative, liberating community. As prototype of Christian baptism, the story places a woman as the central actor, as both priest and prophet. She becomes not only paradigmatic "true disciple,"[65] but also paradigmatic liturgical presider, acting on behalf of the community, expressing its faith in the Anointed One, acting as agent of the Divine, engaged in the ongoing work of building the Messianic community. Finally, this liturgical reclamation and reconstruction is necessary because it is faithful. The memory of this woman's liturgical-prophetic act must be recovered, as a witness to the legitimacy and value of women's memory, women's prophecy, women's liturgical agency. We can only imagine what Christianity would look like if all baptismal anointings were performed "in memory of her." The use of this baptismal prototype as resource for prayer texts, iconography, and preaching is one way to nurture our liturgical imaginations and move the church toward a recovery of that lost memory, that something missing.

CHAPTER THREE

"A WHOLE NEW POETRY BEGINNING HERE"

Emancipatory Language

Christian liturgy is not solely concerned with memory and imagination. For both of these activities, even when entered into communally, as they are in liturgy, are not of themselves oriented toward change, although both are necessary in order for change to come about. But at the heart of liturgy is change indeed, or what in theological terms is called *metanoia,* conversion, transformation. This process of transformation is central to the liturgy because the primary action of liturgy is dialogue. Liturgy is a dialogue with God, an encounter with the one who calls us into community with one another. And as an inevitable result of that encounter, we are changed. Change is always the result of genuine dialogue with another person, since we cannot enter into such dialogue without being open to the perspective of someone other than ourselves. But when the genuine encounter is with God, a profound transformation is called forth.

This is not to say, of course, that every liturgical experience results in transformation for every person present. It is not even to say that every liturgical experience is a genuine encounter with God. It is to say that God is fully present in our liturgical celebrations; it is we who are sometimes absent, or reluctant, or resistant to opening ourselves to the transforming dialogue with God which lies at the heart of Christian liturgy. A dialogue always requires two participants.[1]

Two conclusions follow from the assertion that the character of liturgy is dialogical. First, it means that change is indigenous to the liturgy. Far from being committed to preserving the status quo or being a conservative force, as liturgy is sometimes called, it is in the nature of liturgy to call forth change, since God calls forth change. If liturgy has seemed to be, or has actually become, a force preserving the state of things as they are (or even as they mighty once have been), it is due to our human resistance to change and not to the nature of Christian liturgy itself. Second, dialogue presupposes a relationship based, at least minimally, on some common ground or shared assumptions, and on mutual respect and participation. But what common ground can possibly be supposed between God and humankind? Our basis as Christians for claiming such a relationship with God is the Incarnation. We claim, however incredible it may seem, that God elected to establish common ground with us by taking on our human condition in the person of Jesus Christ. This is why, quite simply, Christians have traditionally prayed "in the name of Jesus," or, in the classical formulation, "to God through Christ in the Holy Spirit." Jesus Christ, as our "common ground", makes dialogue with God possible.

Because liturgy has this dialogical character, then, language is deeply important to it. This concern is often addressed as the centrality of the Word in Christian liturgy, but it is critical not to confuse the Word with inanimate words. For as the term *dialogue* suggests, the emphasis is not on the word in itself, but the word as active. Obviously the liturgy engages in a level of communication that goes beyond the bare exchange of words: the word spoken and heard and touched, the word sung and danced and prayed; the word embodied and gestured and seen in vision and in art, even the word which exists in silence. The fact that God incarnate in Jesus Christ is called the Word witnesses to the depth of the conversation which is implied in the Christian use of the term *Word*.

THE FEMINIST CRITIQUE OF LANGUAGE

This is the context in which the awareness of the inadequacy of androcentric language has arisen. Although the debate about the use of inclusive language in liturgy has often seemed to focus narrowly on words rather than the Word in the full christological and liturgical sense outlined above, the intensity of the emotions and commitments the debate has evoked suggests that indeed we are dealing with something deeper than just words.

On one level, the critique of exclusive male language in liturgy is no different from a critique of exclusive male language in, say, textbooks or the newspaper or in public discourse of any kind. That is to say, any use of androcentric language renders women invisible. This has philosophical, moral, and semantic implications. The philosophical implications suggest that women are at best insignificant, at worst secondary to and derivative from the normal human being, the man. Thus it is implied that women are abnormal or not fully human. The moral implications of the invisibility of women lie in the ability of language to create what it names. Invisible women have no voice, make no claims for themselves, possess no rights, exercise no moral agency. And the use of androcentric language makes the truth of whatever is said suspect, since women are in fact not invisible.

But to make the claim that liturgical language (which is language in the richest sense of the term) is androcentric is to challenge the authenticity of that liturgical dialogue with God which gives shape to the liturgy. It also challenges the accuracy of the claim that the liturgy is the work of the people when so many of the people are rendered invisible and silent.[2] At stake, then, are the church's relationship with God and the church's understanding of its own work. Having stated the situation in these terms we can begin to see why the subject of inclusive language in church generates such strong feeling on both sides and why it is a subject of more than linguistic interest.

Because of the richness of the use of the Word in Christian liturgy and in theological discourse, a variety of liturgical activities are implied with its use, as we have already suggested. We may identify particular ones whose authenticity is called into question by a critique of the use of androcentric language. The appropriate translation of the Scriptures continues to be a subject of serious scholarship, as does the authentic interpretation of them in the act of preaching. Especially, the demand on the one hand to depict as accurately as possible the patriarchal assumptions of the biblical texts and the need on the other to allow the Scriptures to speak to the present context present Scripture scholars with a formidable task.[3] Feminist biblical scholars raise another problem in relation to Scripture's role in liturgy and in particular its authoritative status. The androcentric and patriarchal character of the Bible makes its use in liturgy problematic from a feminist perspective. Since these are authority issues which are separable from the language issues, we shall deal with them separately in the chapter on the Bible and preaching.

A second problem identified by this critique is the problem of God-language. Since liturgy speaks both about and to God, the liturgy has always sought clarity as well as beauty in its language about God. The feminist critique that our traditional liturgical God-language is exclusively male charges that such language is in fact not clear because it is not truthful, and not beautiful because it is oppressive. This critique also observes that the use of such limited language constricts our relationship with the God with whom we dialogue, and thus, in this sense, also does damage to the liturgical act. To put it another way, the use of solely male language for God implies that there is "common ground" between God and men which does not exist between God and women. Although this problem is certainly related to the broader questions about liturgical language in general, we shall postpone it until the next chapter, where we may consider it more fully.

Although it may appear that in postponing discussions of the Bible and of God-language we have left very little to consider, in fact what remains is the verbal language of prayer, of song, of acclamation, of creed; the kinesthetic language of gesture, of posture, of movement; and the visual language of art, icon, and space. The feminist critique of these aspects of liturgy will be examined and their emancipatory possibilities considered.

CONSTRUCTING EMANCIPATORY LANGUAGE

There are three possible ways to respond to the problem of androcentric liturgical language. Although these three approaches are distinct, they are in practice often found together, and thus do not necessarily imply opposing viewpoints on the subject of sexist language. The three ways we shall call nonsexist, inclusive, and emancipatory. Although the terms nonsexist language and inclusive language are widely used, they are often used interchangeably. For clarity of the discussion, however, I propose to identify them with different solutions to the problem of sexist language. Nonsexist language seeks to avoid gender-specific terms. Inclusive language seeks to balance gender references. Emancipatory language seeks to transform language use and to challenge stereotypical gender references.

Nonsexist language, as the term implies, accomplishes its goal by substituting sex-blind terms wherever possible. For example, *people* or *humanity* would be preferred to *men*. In some cases this approach has worked to the enrichment of our use of language. The use of *people* or *humanity*, for example, may be understood to include not only women but also children, both of whom are implicitly excluded from the understood meaning of the term *men*. This is precisely the intention of this solution: to expand the possibilities of meaning beyond those implied by the use of male generic terms. At the same time, however, this avoidance of gender-specific language can impoverish our use of language as well. When human characteristics (although not necessarily sexuality) are no longer applied to inanimate objects or collectives in a poetic or metaphorical way, some imaginative richness is lost. Although the use of such language, such as the church as "bride," unquestionably carried profoundly limiting patriarchal implications, the inability to use female language as representative of something human and at the same time beyond human is a loss. A genderless world, especially in the imagination, is rather flat and colorless.

In particular, theological problems arise in connection with language about God and Jesus, where uncertainty about the

63

theological significance of gender becomes particularly acute. However, the nonsexist solution would still prefer to avoid gender-specific language where possible, normally by avoiding the use of pronouns in reference to either Jesus or God, and by using nongender-specific titles for each, such as *Sovereign* rather than *Lord,* or *Child of God* rather than *Son of God.*[4] Related to this dilemma is that posed by the traditional trinitarian formula. Nonsexist solutions to this problem, however, rather than employing gender-neutral relational terms (*Parent, Child* for *Father, Son*) have resorted instead to functional language, most commonly *Creator, Redeemer, Sustainer.*[5] A partially nonsexist model has been proposed by Gail Ramshaw-Schmidt, who suggests the terms *Abba, Servant, Paraclete.* In this proposal, only the first person of the trinity remains gender-specific, and only to those who recognize *Abba* as the Aramaic intimate term for father.[6]

The nonsexist approach offers many advantages in the search for an adequate alternative to androcentric language. To those already mentioned may be added its relative modesty and lack of disruption of familiar language. As more general terms such as *humankind* are widely accepted, their introduction into liturgical language is relatively untraumatic. However, a serious difficulty with the use of nonsexist language in general is the tendency for hearers to interpret nongender-specific language as male. That is, in patriarchal and androcentric society, in which the male is the norm, this norm is supported by more than language. Not only long linguistic habit but daily experience encourages the hearing of male reality as normative, even when it is not specifically stated. There are other difficulties as well when nonsexist language is employed in translation or interpretation of a text (since it is possible that an author who uses *man* may really mean *man* and not *humanity*). But for our present purposes the problem of androcentric hearing of nonsexist language poses the most serious drawback to its use, given the imaginative character of liturgy.

Inclusive language recognizes this problem with nongender-specific language and answers it by including female references explicitly, normally balanced with male references. In place of the indeterminate *one* or *person,* inclusive language will use *her or she;* or rather than *humanity,* it will prefer *women and men* or *brothers and sisters.* The purpose here is to make explicit the inclusiveness which is implicit in nonsexist language. Rather than seeking to avoid gender-specific language, inclusive language seeks to balance gender language so that both male and female references are included. This approach not only restores color and clarity to language, it also encourages the inclusion of names of women to balance the names of men, which appear far more often in the liturgy.[7]

The weakness of this approach lies in its assumption that male and female images are symmetrical. In fact, both linguistically and socially, women and anything associated with women is devalued. In theological language, this becomes immediately apparent when one begins to search for female parallels to traditional terms of respect and authority assigned to God or to God's representatives. *Queen* is not parallel to *King,* even if one sets aside the homophobic use of *queen; Lady* is not parallel to *Lord* in common use; *Mother* carries wholly different connotations from *Father; Madam* conveys negative associations absent from *Sir; Mistress* has almost nothing in common with its linguistic parallel, *Master;* and so on.[8]

This social and linguistic asymmetry is not addressed and may even be disguised by the use of inclusive or balanced language. What the asymmetry reveals, of course, is the way that language functions as both a creator and sustainer of social structure. In this case, the social structure is patriarchal and androcentric, and therefore the balance sought by the inclusive model is impossible without social change as well as linguistic change.

It is this recognition of the interconnection between language and social system which motivates the third model, that of emancipatory language. Although this is my own term, the practice of using language to challenge and transform language itself is not my own invention. Racial minority groups in this country in particular have used language this way, by claiming degraded terms and making them terms of pride and power. The most obvious examples of this are the transformation of *black* and *chicano/chicana* into terms of pride. Similarly, the women's movement has claimed the word *woman* and transformed it from its former impolite meaning into a term of pride. Consider this definition of *woman* from a recent handbook on writing: "Used as a noun, *woman* connotes independence, competence, and seriousness of purpose as well as sexual maturity."[9] The claiming of this term in a theological context is evident, for example, in the choice of the term *women-church* to refer to women's communities of prayer and ritual.[10]

This emancipatory use of the language has two foci. One already noted is the reappropriation and reinterpretation of terms of derision or shame as terms of pride and strength. A second is the use of such language to create collective identity for a group which has lacked such an identity and may be divided against itself. It is this connection between women which is the goal of the "common language" of which Adrienne Rich dreams: "two women, eye to eye / measuring each other's spirit, each other's / limitless desire, / a whole new poetry beginning here."[11] This woman-to-woman connection is emphasized in the use of the terms *women-church,* or "*ekklesia* of women," defined as "the gathering of women as a free and decision-making assembly of God's people."[12] Thus for women, who have been systematically silenced, this claiming of not only speech (whether liturgical/theological or poetic) but also the power to create language is profoundly emancipatory. Emancipatory language wishes to invoke language-creating power as a solution to the problem of androcentric language.

Theologically, each solution implies a slightly different view of the relationship between God and humanity. Nonsexist language suggests that God does not regard our gender, or that our gender is not relevant to our relationship with God. Inclusive language implies that God does regard our gender, but that both women and men possess equal status before God. Emancipatory language assumes that God is engaged in women's struggles for emancipation, even to the point of identifying with those who struggle. Since liturgy operates on many levels of understanding, all of these views may be found in liturgy at some point. For example, a Scripture text may be genuinely addressed to all members of the community, without distinction of gender. The baptismal rite, particularly in the ancient church when it included baptism in the nude, witnesses to gender inclusivity, with its radical affirmation of equality among Christians. A prayer which names sexism as sin is emancipatory.

However, in spite of the interconnections of these three modes of dealing with androcentric language, both nonsexist and inclusive language approaches have their weaknesses. Within limited circumstances they both have uses, but emancipatory language is necessary in order to move beyond the limits of androcentric language to the generation of a new vision and a new way of speaking about that vision. Such speaking is necessary in order to bring the vision to reality. If androcentric language fails because it makes women invisible, then emancipatory language must make women visible. What are the characteristics of this language, and how is it to be used in the celebration of liturgy?

It should be noted here that although the term *language* normally means verbal language, in the context of a discussion of liturgy we must also take into account the importance of nonverbal language, namely, physical language (or body language) and visual language (the use of space and images). We shall consider each of these different aspects of language separately, but in reality they are experienced simultaneously, and thus the distinction is largely a conceptual one.

VERBAL EMANCIPATORY LANGUAGE

Emancipatory language makes women visible. First of all, then, such language necessarily refers to women directly and specifically, to women as individuals (by name if possible) and to women as a group. As obvious as this sounds, it is surprisingly difficult to do for anyone trained, as we all are, in the use of androcentric language. The first step, then, is to make oneself aware of the existence of women in the church and in the world, and then to name that awareness. This is the truth-telling aspect of emancipatory language. In part it depends on the recovery of women's memory. In part it depends on our willingness to look honestly at women's experience in the present, both in and beyond the church.

As in the recovery of women's memory, there is much to mourn in women's experience in the present. One need only look at the physical, sexual, and psychological abuses, which are daily realities for millions of women and daily threats to all women, to begin to grasp the enormity of what it would mean to speak the truth about women's experience.[13] Lament is a fitting response, not only because of what women have suffered in the past, but also because of the daily suffering of women. But when we begin to see this suffering reality, we also begin to recognize that in the present, as in the past, women are not only victims. The courage and resourcefulness of women who struggle against and survive this suffering deserve celebration. Thus the honesty characteristic of emancipatory language demands both the lament and the celebration of women by name and of women as a group.

Language that is honest and specific about the reality of women's experience cannot indulge in romanticism or sentimentality. Both are forbidden by the hard reality of women's lives. Theologically, this suggests that we resist the temptation to speculate about the "femininity" of God, Jesus, the Holy Spirit, or human males, or to develop "spiritualized" notions about women's experiences of motherhood or sexuality. Motherhood as institution and female sexuality as defined and controlled by patriarchal culture are the source of much of women's suffering, even though our experiences of motherhood and our own sexuality are also often a source of courage and an aid to survival.[14]

Language that makes women's experience visible must therefore recognize the physical realities of women's lives. This means not only acknowledging the fact that women are born physically at risk for abuse in our society, but also taking seriously women's embodiment. That women are capable of conceiving children, giving birth to them, and nurturing them from our bodies affects all women, whether we bear and nurse children or not. We cannot, however, immediately conclude from this reality that women's generative and nurturant abilities are a source of power for women, although we might be able to imagine that in a completely different society they might be. Nor can we simply equate women's ability to bear and nurse children with God's activity in the world or in relation to humanity unless we are willing to say that God, like most women, is coerced or forced into bearing children against her will or for purposes other than her own.

Because of the church's habitual fear and abhorrence of women's bodies and their functions, our language, especially our theological language, has either obscured or romanticized women's physical reality. Therefore emancipatory language seeks ways of speaking which are not limited to identifying women by our sexual function (such as virgin, mother, or wife). It seeks ways of speaking which foster respect and love for women's bodies in place of fear and hatred. This need, deeply felt by many women, has motivated the generation of rites and liturgies that sacralize women's typical bodily experiences such as menstruation, childbirth, and menopause, or which address the bodily violation often experienced by women in rape or battering.[15]

Honesty about women's experience also confronts us with those social structures that divide women from women, especially divisions of class and race as well as religion. The tendency of white, western, well-educated women to attempt to speak for all women is not an emancipatory impulse and must be confronted wherever it appears. Traditional theological language has preferred to transcend racial, class, and gender distinctions by appealing to supposed universal categories of experience. But such categories, in fact based on the experience of white western men, have been challenged by theologians representing third world perspectives—black perspectives, Hispanic perspectives, Asian perspectives—as well as women's perspectives from the same varieties of cultures and traditions. Emancipatory language cannot claim universal human experience as its basis without denying the diversity of human experience as well as the social and political realities that divide us. Moreover, the use of universalized language not only denies our diversity, but also obscures the reality that some of us benefit from the oppression and suffering of others, and that women can be found on both sides of that equation.[16]

Emancipatory language, then, must engage in truth-telling about women's experience. It must reflect the struggles of women for survival and dignity without resorting to romanticism or spiritualizing. This truth-telling (whether the truth of the past or the truth of the present) calls forth both lament for unnecessary suffering and loss and celebration of courage and beauty where they are found. This is language that names women, both of past and present, by naming their experience. Emancipatory language rejects the anonymity of women and declines to participate in it. This language also recognizes and speaks of women's physical experience without fear or hatred.

With this truth-telling as a necessary prerequisite, emancipatory language can then move to the imaginative construction of powerful and positive language about women. Such language is necessarily visionary and prophetic, and may need to transcend the limits of patriarchal and androcentric language. Like the Hebrew prophets' vision of the Messianic age of peace and restoration, or like the Christian apocalyptist vision of the New Jerusalem, emancipatory language must also reveal something of what we might be, as an alternative to present suffering, as a goal toward which to move, and as a future to anticipate. Liturgically, this means seeing the healing of women's wounds, the cessation of hatred and abuse of women, the restoration to women of our past and our memories, the full and free participation of women in the world, and in the shaping and interpreting of life in the world as part of the eschatological fulfillment toward which we move.

Because the liturgy is an eschatological as well as anamnetic activity, this vision of fulfillment for women must take liturgical shape and must inform the liturgy. In our liturgical action the assembly anticipates the fulfillment of all God's promises and celebrates a foretaste of this coming age. The traditional language of fulfillment has needed to transcend normal language to evoke visions of plentiful and unending banquets and feasts, of a city made of precious stone which houses a people who no longer suffer, of trees of life and healing, of rivers of life and abundance. Emancipatory language likewise must explore the limits of visionary speech. And as the presbyter John spoke of what he saw in terms of what he knew (city, tree, river, throne), emancipatory language must speak in terms of what we know of women's lives—embodiment, particularity, suffering and struggle, abuse and terror. It should also speak of the visionary future when all women will be healed, transformed, and restored to fullness. But before we can begin to speak of what we see, we must learn to see.

VISUAL EMANCIPATORY LANGUAGE

Although the presbyter John saw his vision of "new heavens and new earth" by means of a spiritual sense—he says he was "in the Spirit"—the ability to be open to new spiritual ways of seeing is related to what we see visually. Margaret Miles has argued that visual images, which surround us daily, help to shape our moral values. Moreover, she notes, these daily images are, by virtue of most western churches' disinterest in or rejection of religious images, entirely secular both in origin and in content. These images originate in the secular media of advertising, television, and newspapers, and are oriented toward secular values of immediate gratification and individual happiness.[17] Because these and other values run counter to the values professed by Christianity, Miles argues, we need to train ourselves "to choose and use images," both by becoming critical of the omnipresent media images and by exposing ourselves to a variety of intentionally chosen images over time.[18]

Media images of women are degrading. This fact has been documented by sociologists and challenged by feminist activists to very little effect. The images of women which confront us all daily in the media continue to show women as foolish, helpless, and dependent, or sometimes the reverse, as domineering, cruel, and evil. Women's sexuality is especially exploited, often objectified as if it were a commodity or a product, often connected with violence and hatred. Women reported about in news media most often play subsidiary roles as wives or mothers of important people, and as people who do not participate in the "real world." Miles' three-step process of "visual training" can be useful to the development of emancipatory visual language.

The first step she proposes is to become conscious of the messages of the images with which we live. For our purposes, this means becoming aware of the images of women portrayed in television and newspaper advertisements, on billboards and other public places, in television and newspaper reporting and entertainment, and in film. It also means making ourselves aware of the images of women portrayed in religious contexts: in church art, publications, newspapers, and so forth. As Miles notes, this may be done either by scanning images quickly to acquire a sense of mutually reinforcing images, or by examining some images closely and slowly. The result of this process of making ourselves aware of the images of women in the media is a kind of "consciousness raising," a bringing into conscious awareness that which is so common as to be ordinarily accepted without question. Once these messages are brought into our consciousness, we are able to analyze and evaluate them critically. It might be added that although one can benefit from reading the studies of others on these images and how they function, the process Miles proposes constitutes a kind of spiritual discipline, and thus must be experiential as well as cognitive.

The second step then is critical personal reflection. The messages must be evaluated not only in the abstract, but also in light of their effect on me as a person, on me as a woman. How do these images inform my perception of myself and of other women? How do the messages carried by these images shape my own and other women's actions in the world and in the church? As a result of these two steps, Miles suggests that we may conclude that a "visual fast" is necessary in order to purify our vision from self-destructive images and messages.

The third step, which may occur in conjunction with the first two, is the intentional choosing of images with which to live. Here our challenge is to discover images that not only touch or please us, but that also offer an alternative moral vision to that offered by the popular media. This means seeking out visual images of women that reject patriarchal models and express an emancipatory vision of women. As in the case of emancipatory

Mother and Daughter by Meinrad Craighead in *The Mother's Songs,* Paulist Press, 1986. Copyright © by Meinrad Craighead, 1986. Reproduced by permission.

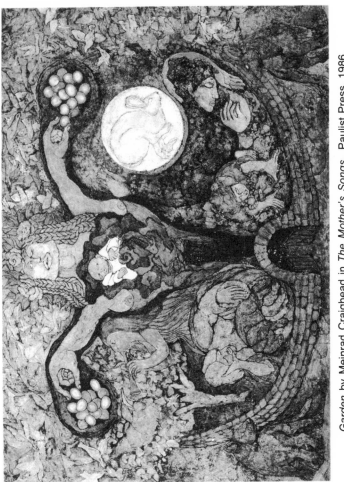

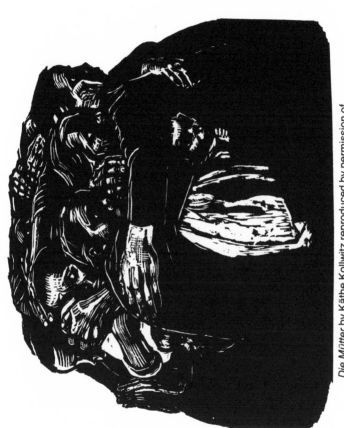

verbal language, these include images that are honest as well as images that are prophetic and visionary.

By way of example, let us consider the images created by two twentieth-century women artists. The drawings of Käthe Kollwitz exemplify the honesty about women's lives that is demanded by emancipatory visual language. Working in Germany during the late nineteenth and early twentieth centuries, Kollwitz produced drawings, etchings, and woodcuts of great power and drama, which depict the world of her time through the eyes of working-class people, especially women. Looking at Kollwitz's women, one sees not only the joys of motherhood depicted in her mother-and-child studies but also the wordless grief of women whose children suffered and died from war and poverty. An especially passionate theme for her was the anguish of women unable to protect their children from the horrors of war. In discussing a poster she was working on in 1924 for the International Trade Union Federation, entitled "The Survivors," depicting a mass of women sheltering their children, Kollwitz noted that she wanted to include the caption, "We did not bear our children for war."[19] Kollwitz's women are strong and solid; they express anguish over deaths of children and husbands; signs of the struggle to survive show on their faces and in their stooped bodies and large worn hands. They are not always defeated, however; some are powerful, muscular, and energetic figures, active participants in revolutionary uprisings, such as the subjects in "The Peasant War" cycle, showing a workers' rebellion.

A more contemporary example of a visionary artist who possesses an emancipatory vision is Meinrad Craighead, whose collection of paintings is published under the title *The Mothers' Songs: Images of God the Mother.*[20] Unlike Kollwitz's work, Craighead's paintings are intentionally religious art, although not conventionally Christian. The scenes depicted have a dreamlike quality, and frequently express an intricate interconnection between female figures, animals, and the natural world. The women in Craighead's paintings are solid and strong-looking, much like Kollwitz's. But the anguish of Kollwitz's women is absent. The women float, dreaming, or are transformed into trees, rivers, shells, angels, flowers. But all of her female figures exude a sense of hieratic power. The world that this work creates celebrates the holiness of women's bodies as sources not only of life and nourishment, but also of connectedness with others (especially other women) and with the earth and its creatures.[21]

The conscious critique of ubiquitous media images of women and the election of alternative honest and visionary images in their place are steps necessary to the creation of emancipatory visual language. The importance of such visual images for liturgy should need no defense; however, in light of the lack of importance placed on visual imagery in most western Christian traditions, perhaps such is necessary. Liturgical use of visual images of women, like verbal images, is distorted by a patriarchal church. One cannot rule out the fact that women may perceive, in traditional female religious images, meanings that run counter to the purposes of patriarchy. However, what few female images exist are intended to reinforce patriarchal values of female submission, female sexual repression, and in general female heteronomy. The submissive female saint of western Christian art is hardly a model of emancipation. In place of such images, or in the virtual absence of any female images, we must choose a variety of different images which depict women honestly, in all our particularity, and eschatologically, in view of what we might be.

Miles speaks of the importance of visual images for liturgy in terms of the ability of the visual image to call forth contemplation from the viewers. This contemplation, or *theoria,* is a process in which the viewer "is lifted out of one's familiar world and into the living presence of the spiritual world" by means of "trained and concentrated seeing."[22] The purpose of emancipatory contemplation, then, is to lift the viewer out of the present patriarchal world into an eschatological or spiritual world in which all women are free. Or, to put it differently, contemplation of emancipatory visual images makes it possible for the trained viewer to see behind and beyond patriarchal distortions and to see with women's eyes.

We have taken as our guiding metaphor in this discussion of language the idea of liturgy as dialogue or encounter, not only with one another but also with God. Distortion of the dialogue occurs when some members of the group are silenced, when they are rendered invisible, or when their images are dishonest or harmful. What is at stake, then, is not values alone, but our relationship with God, since by contemplation of visual images as well as by use of verbal language we enter into dialogue with God.

PHYSICAL EMANCIPATORY LANGUAGE

Liturgy inevitably involves physical movement of various kinds. Those who worship are physical, embodied beings, not pure disembodied spirit. We bring our bodies with us when we worship. Moreover, the active, participatory nature of liturgy itself demands action and physical participation. Then too, a religion based on Incarnation as a leading theological conviction cannot be reduced to verbal expression alone. The Word is not reducible to words. So together with consideration of verbal language and visual language we must also take up the question of physical language, or, as it is often called, *body language.*

Nonverbal behavior is a major medium of human communication, and as psychologist Nancy Henley notes, power is a major topic of discussion. In *Body Politics: Power, Sex, and Nonverbal Communication* Henley studies closely the nonverbal ways in which human beings establish and maintain dominance. Many of Henley's observations about social and public interaction have application to the nonverbal element of liturgy. Her observations can help us to evaluate the physical language we use in liturgy and to construct emancipatory physical language.[23]

Many of the nonverbal behaviors we use daily have a dual function. They can serve either as symbols of intimacy or as symbols of dominance, depending on whether the relation between the individuals involved is symmetrical or asymmetrical. Between equals, such behavior as eye contact, personal forms of address, touching, and relaxed posture denotes intimacy. But between superior and subordinate, only the superior has the right to make and maintain eye contract or to stare, to use a familiar form of address, to touch, or to assume a relaxed posture. The subordinate, by contrast, is expected to drop or avert the eyes modestly, to use respectful or polite address, to accept but not initiate touch, and to maintain a formal posture.[24] In the absence of or in addition to such gestures of dominance, symbols are also used to denote dominance. The chief of these are the use of greater height, either bodily height or constructed height; the wearing of authoritative clothing; and the use of symbols of office, especially official space.[25]

Evidently, most liturgical actions and gestures have more in common with gestures and symbols of dominance than of intimacy or equality. The clergy occupy official sacred space, which is often also physically elevated above the congregation. The clergy are also elevated when they stand while the congregation sits. Clergy may wear authoritative clothing or other symbols of authority. They are regarded as having the license to address parishioners by familiar names while being themselves addressed by title. Similarly, clergy normally touch parishioners in the course of religious rites or as part of their more general pastoral duties. Lay people do not normally touch their clergy, beyond a polite handshake, and may feel some degree of anxiety if expected to do so.

Operating at a level below the fully conscious, then, many of the gestures, postures, and movements we use in liturgy work to establish and maintain relations of dominance and submission. It is worth noting at this point that many of the difficulties, that clergywomen report experiencing, can be understood as reactions to the jarring experience of having a woman in a position of dominance. Henley lists the following possible responses to a woman who uses gestures or symbols of dominance: (1) she may be ignored; (2) her actions may be denied, particularly by being reinterpreted as sexually inviting (this generates great conflict in Christians who have been conditioned to regard sexuality as dangerous or at least nonreligious, as is evidenced by complaints by men that women ministers are simply too "distracting"); (3) her actions may be punished, either physically or, more often in church contexts, psychologically, by labeling her as "deviant and abhorrent, castrating bitch, lesbian," or by challenging her calling to the ministry or her theological orthodoxy; (4) her actions may be accepted at face value, which normally means that she will be met with open expressions of anger, and that attempts to restore the "normal" pattern of male dominance will be made; (5) her actions may elicit acquiescence, showing signs of recognizing the legitimacy of her authority in this instance.[26]

Emancipatory body language must work to eliminate gestures and symbols of dominance from the liturgy and to generate symbols and gestures of mutuality and egalitarianism. At stake here is a principle dear to both the liturgical movement and the feminist movement, that of the full and free participation of the whole people of God in their liturgical work. Symbols and gestures of dominance work against the realization of this goal. The problem is how to create gestures of mutuality that can still serve the public, formal requirements of liturgical activity. As Henley has observed, some gestures of dominance and submission can become gestures of intimacy when used between equals. Theologically (although certainly not actually) the church has asserted that all members of the Body of Christ are equal. Thus we may begin by proposing the elimination of gestures and symbols that do not admit of this equality, or that cannot be made reciprocal. The existence of barriers or restrictions of access to any space for appropriate purposes works against the equality of the baptized. This would naturally include anything which would prevent access by the physically challenged. Similarly, space elevated beyond the practical needs of visibility and audibility would be disallowed. One may also question whether special seating for some members of the community other than what might be needed for practical reasons has any place in an emancipatory community. Use of clothing or other symbolic vesture, which is intended to denote status or rank rather than service to and within the community, is also problematic, since most of liturgical dress used now has origins in signs of civil rank or social status at the time the church became legalized under Constantine. At the same time, one is reluctant to eliminate liturgical dress entirely, since it can assist our sense of the sacred and of drama, and since contemporary street clothes are so unlovely. What is needed, it seems, is the creation (or reconstruction) of liturgical garments that enhance the dramatic and hieratic character of liturgy without employing symbols of rank or status.

Gestures of dominance, which inhibit the experience of the equality of all the members of the community, are those which are used asymmetrically. The giving of blessings by one person only, disproportionate speaking while others are silent, standing while others are silent, standing while others are sitting, and especially standing while others kneel, are gestures that by their asymmetry denote relations of dominance and submission. In their stead reciprocal gestures and symmetrical postures can be used. In fact, the reformed liturgies already include an ancient example of an emancipatory gesture that is reciprocal and symmetrical—the kiss of peace. When shared freely among the community rather than clericalized, the kiss of peace becomes a prophetic expression of the emancipatory community the church is called to be.[57]

The purpose of generating gestures and symbols of emancipatory relationships, it should be stated, is not to establish intimacy among the members of the worshiping community, at least not psychological or interpersonal intimacy. Its purpose rather is to seek new forms and patterns of public interaction that do not depend on dominance of one person or group over another. From our interpersonal experiences of genuine mutuality and equality (which are likely to be intimate as well) we may begin to shape our public gestures in ways that will foster equality and freedom as well as solidarity and community.

This brings us back to where this chapter began. Liturgy is ongoing dialogue and relationship between God and the assembly. As in the human realm, that relationship depends on and is shaped by the language used; the gestures, postures, and actions employed; the images invoked and implied. To the extent that women have been excluded not only from participating in this dialogue but also from shaping it and setting its terms, the relationship has been and continues to be flawed. Only the construction of a "whole new poetry" can heal the relationship and recover the fullness of the vision of community with God and one another.

CHAPTER FOUR

"WHEN I SAW HER FACE"

God Language

The liturgical dialogue takes place primarily between God and God's people as present in the gathered community. This dialogical encounter with the living God motivates and shapes our liturgies and our understanding of God. What then can we say about this God whom we encounter in our worship, with whom we establish a relationship by virtue of this encounter, and with whom we enter into dialogue?

This fundamental question has occupied systematic theologians, who have always struggled to express as clearly as possible what we know of the nature of God. From time to time challenges and questions have arisen, both from within the church and from without, concerning the adequacy of a given understanding of God's nature. Theologians have not hesitated to adopt different philosophical frameworks and language to say what is known about God in ways that are adequate to contemporary understanding. In recent times the feminist movement has challenged the adequacy of preferential male language in speaking of God and has proposed new perspectives for developing more adequate language.

The feminist liturgical movement has been raising the question of gendered God-language in an increasingly urgent and articulate way since the beginnings of the movement. The critique itself is simple: exclusively or dominantly male language about God grants authority to men in a patriarchal culture and religion. This is particularly true when titles ascribed to God duplicate those also given exclusively to men, such as father, king, or master. Such titles operate in a dual manner. That is, they suggest not only that God is like a father, or king, or master, but also that fathers, kings, and masters are somehow like God.

An important corollary to the fundamental critique of male God-language is that the absence of female titles or character-istics of God carries the further implication that women are somehow less like God than are men. Thus not only are men granted power by the use of male referents to God, but women are denied legitimate power by the absence of female referents. This denial has carried heavy social and religious disabilities as the association of women, especially women's bodies and their functions, with evil and sin has given rise to restrictions on or rejection of women's exercise of legitimate power.[1] Among other things, this has resulted in the denial of liturgical agency and leadership to women.

This insight into the relationship between religious lan-guage and patriarchal social structures has proven to be foundational in the development of feminist theology. But it is also profoundly significant for liturgical practice and theology. For if exclusively male language about God is inadequate, then our liturgical encounter with God is being impoverished. Equally serious is the implication that our impoverished relationship with God is made to support impoverished human relationships, which further distort our liturgical assemblies. Thus there are ethical as well as theological-litur-gical implications that follow from this insight.

Liturgical response to the feminist critique of male God-language must take into account both this basic insight and its corollary. That is, liturgical language must be reconstructed with an awareness of the limits and dangers of male language and a parallel awareness of the problem of the absence of female language. To resolve one of these problems is not necessarily to resolve the other. The dangers of male God-language, for example, can perhaps be alleviated by avoiding gender-specific language altogether, so that no overt support of human patriarchal structures is implied. But this does not answer the problem of the absence of female God-language. Conversely, we can add female God-language by using female terms in place of or parallel to male terms ("Father-Mother God," for example, or "Mother" in place of "Father"), so that the absence of female language is redressed. But this does not challenge the support of patriarchal structures, and in fact may deepen it by evoking stereotypical female roles and activities in patriarchal society.[2]

GENDER AND SYMBOL

A related observation arising from this basic insight is that gender is a socially constructed reality and that our gender identity therefore affects not only our social and ecclesial roles but also every aspect of our experience, since all human beings are gendered.[33] This observation has profound significance for our use of God-language, since, as Caroline Walker Bynum has indicated, the use of gender in religious symbolic language is complex. "Gender-related symbols, in their full complexity, may refer to gender in ways that affirm or reverse it, support or question it; or they may, in their basic meaning, have little at all to do with male and female roles."[4] At the same time, because these symbols are used by gendered people, their use and interpretation depends on the gender of the persons using and interpreting them. Walker Bynum concludes: "It is not possible ever to ask How does a symbol—*any* symbol—mean? without asking For whom does it mean?"[5]

This recognizes two things important to our discussion of the construction of feminist God-language: First, that all God-language, because it is symbolic language, is complex and polyvalent; second, that the meaning of that symbolic language (whether gendered or not) is shaped by the gender identity of the user of the symbol. It must be added here that as fundamental as gender is to our experience, there are other aspects of cultural location that are equally determinative. I mean by this such constitutive aspects of our identities as race and class, and the particular historical realities that shape the identities of people of different races and different classes. Thus we must ask not only about the gender of the interpreter of the symbol, but also about other pertinent aspects of the interpreter's social location.

This matter of the social location of the symbol interpreter is important for a consideration of the liturgical use of symbols, since in the liturgical context the symbol interpreter is the worshiper in the assembly. Or, to put it more precisely, the liturgy itself interprets the symbol for the assembly, but members of the assembly will appropriate (or reject) that symbol in ways that make sense from within their particular social location. To use Walker Bynum's questions, then, we may ask of the liturgy *how* a symbol has meaning, but we must ask *for whom* a symbol has meaning by taking into account the social location of the worshiper. It is also necessary to recognize the origins of most liturgies. Although in many worship traditions liturgies give the appearance of having divine rather than human origins, in fact they are created by human persons. To the extent that they are "official", that is, designed by, approved by, or written by leaders of a religious group or denomination, they are most likely to be produced by men or at least to reflect male interpretations and support patriarchal interests.

BASIC ISSUES

The fundamental theological question raised anew by the feminist critique of male God-language is, How shall we talk about God? The way in which this question is answered by philosophers, theologians, biblical scholars, and church historians can provide valuable resources for liturgical reconstruction, in that we are enabled to evaluate our liturgical practices in light of philosophical, historical, theological, and biblical scholarship. However, the liturgical question raised by this critique is more urgent and primary: How shall we address God?[6] It is more urgent and primary because liturgy is not reflection but address; an encounter is presumed, and that God is available to be addressed is taken for granted, or is at least the focus of our hope each time we gather in the liturgical assembly.

This dialogical character of liturgy has been discussed in

relation to the way in which we talk about one another and ourselves before God. But liturgy is not only talking (and moving and so forth) *before* God, it is also talking (and moving and so forth) *with* God. Just as in human encounters, we must know how to address the one with whom we intend to dialogue, and we ask, "How do you like to be addressed?" or "What shall I call you?" We could discuss for a long time the proper way to address royalty, but unless we expect to meet any, the discussion remains, so to speak, academic. When we are introduced to the Queen, the question becomes both primary and urgent.

Thus the urgency and primacy of the question of how to address God is in part derived from the encounter character of the liturgy. But it is also primary and urgent because the way in which we address God will shape our relationship with God. The use of titles and honorifics indicate respect and preserve distance between the speakers. Good friends use first names; lovers, parents, and children use affectionate nicknames. Those forms of address help shape the ongoing relationship by reminding the participants of the nature of the relationship and by tacitly indicating what kind of behavior is appropriate and what can be expected. The use of patriarchal titles for God such as Lord, King, and Father indicate what kind of behavior is appropriate for us and what we can expect from God. Patriarchal relationships of dominance and submission are reinforced by such forms of address.

Finally, the question of how to address God is primary and urgent because, as Mary Collins notes, "our liturgical assemblies continue to gather," and the liturgical encounter takes place without waiting on the results of scholarly research.[7]

Feminist liturgists have not waited for theological consensus on the proper form of address for God. Feminist liturgies, responding to the insight regarding the significance of male God-language and to the urgency of their own felt need, have begun to explore alternative possibilities. True to the general feminist liturgical commitment to process over product, this liturgical exploration has generated a rich variety of possibilities but has for the most part resisted claiming that there is only one right way to address God. Because of this commitment to experimentation and tolerance of diversity, it is very difficult to generalize or even to identify "schools" of thought on God-language.[8]

However, one generalization that may be made is that the need to discover appropriate and emancipatory female language for God is deeply felt and actively pursued. The process of experimenting with this language has generated critical reflection on liturgical practice, which has in its turn generated refinement of liturgical practice. This process of critical dialogue has identified pressing theological issues which demand further critical reflection. The search for female language about God raises the critical questions identified in relation to generating emancipatory language about women, namely, the lack of non-patriarchal words for women and our experience.

Some have begun to use the name *Goddess* out of recognition of this difficulty, and this terminology is used both within the Christian feminist liturgical movement and within non-Christian feminism. This usage has raised important historical-critical issues for feminist theology and practice. Some have adopted the use of *Mother* as a name of God (or Goddess), although it carries heavy patriarchal meaning and raises important questions about the extent to which patriarchal symbols can be reinterpreted. Within Judaism and Christianity, the question of monotheism is raised, its problems identified, and its necessity challenged by feminist thought. Similarly, for Christians the problem of trinitarian language is raised and its theoretical and practical problems for feminism identified. All these issues press the question beyond that of what female words can we use to speak of and to God, to questions such as why speak of God as *God,* as *One,* or as *Three-in-One.* An examination of these critical issues can help guide our search for more adequate answers to the question of how to address God in public prayer.

GOD AS FEMALE

Although orthodox Christianity and Judaism have insisted that God is "beyond" (or "above") gender, the use of non-gendered referents for God have proven unsatisfactory from a feminist perspective. There are several reasons for this, including the problem already noted in relation to the use of non-sexist (gender-neutral) language in general, namely that gender-neutral human referents tend to be heard as male unless they are stereotypically female. The use of *God* as if it were gender-neutral does not challenge the prevailing belief that God is male. A further difficulty has been the suspicion generated by the insistence of theologians that *God* is neither male nor female: "*He* is spirit."[9] Gender-neutral language, proposed as a solution to at least half of the problem with the idolatry of male-only God-language, has proven to be of limited use. At best, the gender-neutral use of God avoids giving offense to those who object to male-only God-language. While it may permit an inclusive interpretation, it does not challenge the idolatry of male language, nor does it seriously disturb the relationship between God-language and patriarchal social referents.

However, perhaps the most significant reason for rejecting the gender-neutral answer to the question of how to address God is its inability to speak to women's need to identify ourselves—our lives, our values, our struggles and aspirations—with God. This is not an intellectual search so much as a spiritual one in which women are longing to find "God in themselves" and to "love her fiercely." In her poem "The Images" Adrienne Rich enumerates the painful images of "fear and woman-loathing" that assault our senses, "dismember" us, and leave us "starving for images" in the midst of a "war of the images." But in the midst of her pain she experiences a moment of revelation, of self-recollection: "When I saw hér face, she of the several faces / . . . when I looked into hér world / I wished to cry loose my soul / into her, to become / free of speech at least."[10] The glimpse of a God whose face is like ours opens our imaginations into another world, which is free of "fear and woman-loathing."

Many feminist theologians have recognized that the use of gender-specific language, far from being avoided, rather must be claimed by discovering or constructing female referents for God. The now classical feminist statement of this conviction is

91

formed in Carol Christ's article "Why Women Need the Goddess: Phenomenological, Psychological, and Political Reflections."[11] In this essay, the author argues that only a female diety can legitimate women's power, affirm women's bodies and their cycles, value women's responsible exercise of their own will, and celebrate women's bonds and heritage. Although Carol Christ rejects both Judaism and Christianity, Christian and Jewish feminists have come to similar conclusions while retaining their faith. Rita Gross, in a 1979 article entitled "Female God-Language in a Jewish Context" argues that "the ability to say 'God-She' is the sign of Jewish women's authentic entrance in their own right into the ritual covenant community of Israel, as well as the unexpected resource for Jewish self-understanding that comes with that entrance."[12] Joanmarie Smith argues that the use of female-only referents to God "will have the effect of dramatically exposing us to the exhaustively male character of our image of the Divine, even where we least expect it," thereby freeing us from the limitations of traditional religious language.[13]

In their search for alternative female models for God, Christian feminist theologians have looked in part to the classic sources for Christian theology—scripture, historical tradition, and theological reflection. That these sources have in fact yielded evidence of at least occasional use of female referents for God has strengthened the feminist conviction that such referents are both necessary and constructive, and that there is room within the Christian tradition for female images of God.

Feminist biblical study has recovered, for example, the rich diversity of images for God, which go far beyond those to which we have limited ourselves in our liturgies or in our theological and doctrinal reflection. Although male models still predominate, the use of female images such as mother, midwife, nurse, seamstress, mistress of a household, give legitimacy to the feminist construction of images of God based on women's experience.[14] Perhaps most influential for the construction of feminist liturgies has been the recovery of Wisdom as a biblical model for God. As an aspect of God represented as a woman, Sophia, or Wisdom, personified

God's creative activity in the world as well as God's companionship with humankind. Sophia gave knowledge of God, salvation, and peace to humanity. She sent the prophets and was a friend to humanity. In Christian wisdom theology Jesus is regarded as the one who is sent by Sophia-God and is empowered by her.[15] Wisdom Christology identifies Jesus himself with Sophia, calling all humanity to herself.[16]

Historical research has also identified neglected traditions that have imaged God in female terms, as found in the writings of medieval mystics who were largely unconstrained by dogmatic concerns and in the traditions of early heterodox and later sectarian Christian movements such as the Shakers, who were bold in their ascription of gender to God.[17] In these traditions, God or Jesus could be imaged as "mother," as a way of recognizing God's tenderness, protection, nurture, our absolute dependence on God (as an infant on its mother) and God's creative, generative powers. In some cases, such as some gnostic Christians and the Shakers, the motherhood of God functions as a complement to the fatherhood of God, so that a dualistic anthropology is confirmed and divinized.[18]

Recovery of these scriptural and historical resources has not only supported the search for female images and metaphors for God, but also offered insight into the difficulties of constructing such language. For if the biblical records include female images of God, they are not only vastly outnumbered by male images, they also reflect patriarchal roles and images of women and thus fail to be fully emancipatory. If there are historical examples of female images for God in the Christian tradition, these images often reproduce stereotypical images of women as mothers and remain firmly androcentric. At best these scriptural and historical images modify the male image of God by implying that God has some female characteristics. At worst, they reinforce patriarchal culture by identifying female roles of motherhood with divine patterns.

As Caroline Walker Bynum's revealing study of the use of female imagery for God in medieval religious communities from the twelfth to the fourteenth centuries notes, the use of female imagery by men does not necessarily have anything to do with women, but rather may reflect male (and one might add, patriarchal) assumptions about women's "nature."[19] In particular, she found that Cistercian monks who employed images of Jesus as mother depended on medieval interpretations of motherhood to affirm the affective relationship between the believer and Christ, and assumed the medieval theory of female inferiority to emphasize the condescension of Christ.[20] As she concludes, "it was not women who originated [these] female images of God."[21] Instead, such images are created by men to serve the purposes of men and they remain firmly androcentric. By contrast, she notes that nuns did not use female imagery for God or Christ nearly so often as monks, and that when they did, the images were used to emphasize their authority to teach, to judge, and to administer, in contrast to the stereotypical nurturing images used by the monks.[22] When the image of God as mother is used by medieval religious women, it often implies not only tenderness and consolation, but also discipline, testing, and judgment.[23]

As a result of this and other scholarship we are beginning to discover how complex the project of constructing female images of God in a patriarchal culture will be. Gender is socially constructed within a patriarchal culture, and serves male ends. The dominant religious and cultural heritage we have received defines femaleness as inferior to maleness. All our existing gender images are part of this social-religious culture. How can female images of God that will not reinforce the already existing asymmetry associated with gender be constructed?

This question affects the usefulness of systematic attempts to address the problem of male-centered God-language, as Elizabeth Johnson observes in a helpful article, "The Incomprehensibility of God and the Image of God Male and Female." She identifies three approaches to the task of revision of God-language. The first approach is that of introducing "feminine traits" into the patriarchal symbol of God. The problems of such an approach are many: God remains firmly male; "femininity" is male-defined, usually as "nurturing, gentle, compassionate," which are female traits only in a

stereotypical way; the so-called "feminine traits" are subor-
dinated to "masculine traits" of a male God; by using
patriarchally defined categories such as "femininity," patriarchy is "subtly furthered."[24] The second approach seeks a
"feminine dimension of the divine," often by defining the
third person of the trinity as feminine. Although the orthodox
insistence on the equality of the three persons of the trinity
would seem to make this possibility more appealing than the
first, in fact it suffers from some of the same disabilities as the
other. The use of patriarchal definitions of "femininity" result
in associations of the Holy Spirit with the unconscious, with
nature, with physical creation, or with immanence in general,
so that patriarchal dichotomies between male and female are
maintained. The main disability with both these approaches
lies in their use of patriarchal and androcentric categories of
"masculinity" and "femininity," in which case "femininity" has
little to do with women and everything to do with what men
imagine about women or (perhaps) about themselves. These
proposals confuse "feminine" with female.

The third approach, and that recommended by Johnson, is
what she carefully calls "the image of God male and female." In
this approach, "female images of God" (*not* "feminine") are
used "without embarrassment or explanation."[25] Recalling the
traditions of "ancient religions that worshipped gods and
goddesses," she notes that both male and female deities are not
stereotyped according to gender conventions, but are "equivalent images of the divine."[26] This approach rejects gender
stereotyping and allows for "the fullness of divine power and
care" to be expressed "in a female image."[27]

As Johnson's analysis shows, there are certain obstacles to
the construction of female language for God. These are the
problems associated with the use of restrictive stereotypes,
especially those derived from uncritical use of categories of
"masculinity" and "femininity"; the difficulty of using terms
taken from women's lived experience (such as "mother") in a
way that is free from patriarchal interpretation; and the
temptation to use gender experiences as if they were
"complementary," which is but a variation on the use of

masculine-feminine dichotomy. But, by keeping these risks before our eyes, we can construct emancipatory images of God, which will generate new levels of encounter with the living God.

GOD AS GODDESS

The search for a female face of God has led many feminists to examine religious traditions that have traditionally been regarded as being antithetical to Judaism or Christianity: namely, Goddess religions. This search has motivated a large and rapidly growing body of research that illuminates non-Christian Goddess-centered religions as they existed before Christianity and as they exist now.[28] Such research has challenged a number of assumptions about Goddess-worship, such as the beliefs that such worship was always *orgiastic* or oriented toward *fertility rites,* that the Goddess was always and exclusively associated with the earth and with birth, that Goddess-worship is primitive and associated with agricultural societies, that such religions have low moral standards. In fact, it seems that ancient goddesses appeared in a rich variety of guises, sometimes indeed associated with birth and nature, but also often associated with culture and civilization, or identified as the givers of knowledge and wisdom, or the givers of law and the judge of human behavior.[29] Far from being limited to societies that live "close to the earth," goddesses associated with culture, civilization, law, and order are often identified as the founders or patrons of great cities.[30]

The recovery of these ancient traditions has been motivated not by scholarly curiosity, but by questions posed by feminists about the origins of patriarchal religion. Merlin Stone's study of ancient goddesses was precipitated by pressing contemporary questions: "How did it happen? How did men initially gain the control that now allows them to regulate the world in matters as vastly diverse as deciding which wars shall be fought when to what time dinner should be served?"[31] Feminists who adopt Goddess-worship find in it a resource for feminist spirituality that they have not found in traditional patriarchal religions such as Christianity or Judaism. In "Why Women Need the Goddess," Carol Christ articulated some of the benefits feminists have found in reconstructing a Goddess-centered religion.[32] She identifies four of these: the valuing of female power, the affirmation of the female body, the valuing of female assertion and will, and the celebration of women's bonds and heritage.[33] These and other values attract many women to Goddess religions, and these values are fully consistent with the search for emancipatory female images for God. To what extent, then, can we assert that this movement's image of Goddess avoids the risks we have identified, and what "sympathetic critiques" have been offered to it?

This movement is so diverse that it is very difficult to summarize. However, there are certain commonalties that may be useful to identify. Although this movement is based to a great extent on the recovery of ancient pre-Christian or non-Christian religions, these traditions are used selectively and creatively, and are not considered authoritative, but only suggestive.[34] Based on the archaeological evidence that some form of Goddess-worship preceded patriarchal religion by millennia, some practitioners of Goddess religion have constructed a contemporary religion which centers on the worship of a Goddess or Goddesses (and sometimes Gods as well). Often the Goddess is viewed as having three faces—the Nymph (or Virgin), the Maiden-Mother, and the Crone—and thus is sometimes called the Triple Goddess. These three aspects of the Goddess represent the three ages of women, and reveal as well the natural life cycle of all that lives. The theoreticians of this movement have begun to call their work thealogy, and themselves thealogians, in order to distinguish themselves from those working within patriarchal traditions. Thealogian Emily Culpepper identifies several weaknesses with much of Goddess thealogy, and offers such critique in the spirit of sympathetic engagement with the religion and/or its practices.

First, while she observes that the sources used by practitioners are diverse, and are typically freely explored, nevertheless there seem to be certain writings that have influenced

Goddess-worship more than others, which Culpepper identifies as the works of Jung on archetypes and Erich Neumann's
The Great Mother. The reliance on this perspective has
constrained, to some extent, the possible diversity of images
for the Goddess. Culpepper notes that the influence of these
and other similar thinkers has generated an overriding image
of the Goddess as the Mother. Thus the Goddess's primary
image is that of "Creatrix of the universe," the Great Mother
who not only gives birth, but also is identified with activities of
mothering, such as giving care, nurturing, teaching, strengthening, giving encouragement, and so on. When this metaphor
is extended to "Mother Earth," it serves also to express our
dependence on the earth itself and our interconnectedness
with all forms of life. While recognizing the great strengths
and importance of this image for many women, Culpepper
also identifies its problems. First of these is the problem of
identifying women too exclusively with motherhood, and
thereby running the risk of confirming patriarchal limitations
on women's lives. As Culpepper observes:

> Archetypes of "Woman" or "Femininity" or "The Mother" are
> too easily compatible with oppressive gender roles. Separating
> reality into male and female essences, however dramatically or
> mythically conceived, ultimately creates only a cosmic rational-
> ization for sex role stereotyping. Archetypal theory of this sort
> collapses the rich diversity of living into a familiar gender
> dualism. When this happens, important realities of women's
> lives begin to fade from view.[35]

By the excessive use of archetypes, Culpepper argues, the
idea becomes more important than real women and the
realities of their lives. She names this "generic erasure," and
identifies several distortions which result. (1) "All women are
not mothers," and the Mother Goddess image fails to
recognize women's choice in bearing or not bearing children;
(2) "birth is an inadequate symbol for many forms of
creativity," and may be used to devalue other forms of female
creativity; (3) "the Great Mother obscures the presence of
lesbians and heterosexism," since even though there are many
lesbian mothers, motherhood in our culture is associated

with heterosexuality; (4) "the Great Mother inadequately challenges the model of female self-sacrifice" in its emphasis on caregiving and nurture; (4) "The Mother Goddess obscures the presence of single women, of spinsters," by focusing exclusively on motherhood; (5) "Goddess monotheism is not new enough" in that it often may duplicate God the Father monotheism and its attendant dualism; (6) "the Goddess is too easily a white Goddess," which is surely the most devastating effect not only of monotheism (as Culpepper notes) but also of the use of dichotomous archetypes of ideal female existence that fail to attend to the lives of real women, especially women of color.[36] A further distortion, which Culpepper fails to note, is the anti-Jewish perspective which blames Judaism for the destruction of Goddess religion and for the creation of patriarchal religion.[37]

To counter these problems in thealogy, Culpepper urges intentional and conscious pluralism, which "is less likely to erase or romanticize vital aspects of women's lives. . . and more likely to help us to recognize our differences as positive."[38]

Because Culpepper has identified so clearly the most urgent problems with the construction of female God-language, we shall return to her arguments in the context of further evaluation of God as Mother, God as One, and God as Plural. However, there are questions about the viability of Goddess-worship that must be raised from within the context of Christian worship: To what extent can the images, practices, and assumptions of Goddess-worship, which often defines itself over against Christianity, be appropriated within a Christian context? What is the basis for such an appropriation? How may such images, practices, and assumptions empower women in Christian tradition? In a way this is an ex post facto discussion, since the use of Goddess-worship practices by Christian feminists and the integration of these practices into Christian liturgy is already taking place.[39] Nevertheless, critical reflection on the practice may not only identify problems but also see fruitful intersections previously unrecognized.

The primary basis for borrowing Goddess-worship practices

is that they answer a deeply felt need. To women raised within and identified with traditional Christianity or Judaism, the experience of praying to and encountering a female deity generates a profound shift in perspective. This perspectival shift not only involves a change in one's understanding of and relationship with God, but also one's sense of self, one's relationships with others, one's interpretation of reality in general. For women who are unable to find a female face of God in their own traditions, or for whom such a face has yet to be presented to them with sufficient power, the Goddess tradition, as reconstructed by contemporary feminists, generates positive changes. Among the positive changes some Christian women report upon experiencing Goddess-worship are a new love and appreciation for their own bodies; stronger sense of identity with other women, even those with ideological or theological differences; greater confidence in their own perceptions and intellectual abilities; and a sense of power as something that comes from within themselves rather than granted to them by others.

Perhaps the most significant change is the sense of tradition suggested by the Goddess movement. Merlin Stone begins her study *When God Was A Woman* with the provocative question: "At the very dawn of religion, God was a woman. Do you remember?"[40] Although we in fact don't remember, we want to. The remembering then becomes imaginative remembering, an intentional restructuring of our collective memory to include the experience of God as a woman. For women accustomed to appeals to tradition from Christian and Jewish religious leaders, the ability to call on a tradition in which God is a woman is powerful and necessary. It is important to note at this point that the tradition of Goddess-worship being evoked is not necessarily historical tradition, but mythic tradition. This is not to say that there is no historical evidence for the preeminence of Goddesses before Gods; in fact there is a great deal of evidence, although we cannot be sure about the social status of women within all Goddess-centered religions. Rather, it is to say that quite aside from the historical questions (which are important in their own right), the tradition invoked by those who worship a Goddess is mythical in the same sense that the Genesis story is mythical; if offers a perspective on the world and the people in it and how it all came to be. As Emily Culpepper observes, "After all, every wave of thinking about the scope of human history has created a vision, a story about early human social arrangements and this often includes creation myths."[41]

Precisely this sense of tradition, however, appears to be problematic for Christian or Jewish feminists. The Goddess tradition often is defined over against patriarchal religions such as Judaism or Christianity, which are blamed for the decline of Goddess worship. Conversely, both Christianity and Judaism have often defined themselves over against so-called "fertility cults" or "paganism," and have at times actively condemned religious practices of those who worshiped Goddesses. How can Christian and Jewish feminists appropriate this tradition, which has apparently been completely rejected by their religions? What possibility for common ground is there? While a full answer to this question would need to go far beyond the limits of this present study, a few comments on possibilities can advance the present discussion.

First, it is worth reminding ourselves that Christianity and Judaism have, at various times in their respective histories, defined themselves over against each other, and that Christians in particular have, to their shame, actively attempted to obliterate Jewish religious practices. Yet it is obvious that Christianity and Judaism grew from a common root; that they exercised a great deal of mutual influence on each other's development; and that Jewish scriptures, beliefs, and religious practices in particular were absorbed into Christianity, Christian attempts to create distance between itself and Judaism notwithstanding. Similarly, Judaism and Christianity both grew up in a religious context that included worship of Goddesses. While similar attempts to create distance between Goddess religions and Judaism or Christianity occurred, scholars have begun to recognize that many aspects of Goddess religions were absorbed and reinterpreted. To take but one example, Pamela Berger, in *The Goddess Obscured*, has studied the ways in which the pre-Christian grain

Goddess, patron to European peasants whose lives depended on the growth of the grain, was reinterpreted first as a Christian saint, eventually being absorbed into the persona of the Virgin Mary.[42] As Berger notes, practices associated with the worship of the grain Goddess persisted among peasants well into the late middle ages, in spite of attempts by the church hierarchy to stop them. Thus, a genuine tradition of Goddess worship seems to have persisted among ordinary Christians for many centuries independently of the church's official cooptation of the Goddess.

Although much more research remains to be done on the influence of Goddess worship on both Christianity and Judaism, it is more than barely possible that such influence existed, and, if identified, can serve as a partial basis for reconstruction of traditional Christianity and Judaism to include worship of God as a woman and to claim traditions of Goddess worship as part of our own.[43]

GOD AS MOTHER

The most frequent female image for God used by Christian feminists as well as those in the Goddess movement is the image of Mother. Within the Christian context, this can be partly accounted for by the predominance of *Father* as a traditional form of address, and the simplicity of substituting the term *Our Mother* for *Our Father*. More ominously, it can also be accounted for by reference to unexamined assumptions about what is essential about women's *nature*, specifically, that we are all mothers, or are meant to be. It may also imply that our ability to bear children makes us as women most godlike. Historian Gerda Lerner names this identification *maternalism* and traces its origins as an idea to the work of J. J. Bachofen in *Das Mutterrecht,* published in 1861, which subsequently influenced Friedrich Engels, Robert Briffault, and later Jungian writers. Bachofen and others held a romantic ideal of the mother-child bond as the basis of all human culture, and posited a matriarchal historical period, which predated patriarchy.[44] Similar ideas were expressed by some nine-teenth-century feminists such as Charlotte Perkins Gilman and Elizabeth Cady Stanton, who argued for women's rights on the basis of women's moral superiority, which derived from women's ability to give birth to children.[45]

While this intellectual tradition may exercise some influence on the Christian feminist use of *Mother* as a name for God, it seems more likely that contemporary (but long-held) beliefs about motherhood have contributed to this use. As Mary Collins notes, "When a presider, in leading the community at prayer, ventures a pronominal 'she' or 'her' to refer to the God of Jesus Christ, it is virtually certain that the prior metaphorical referent has been maternal."[46] Maternal, in this case, normally implies nurture, tenderness, and care. However, these supposed characteristics of motherhood are in fact derived not from women's own experiences of motherhood, but from the ideology of the patriarchal institution of motherhood.[47] The romanticism of such a view of motherhood obscures the painful reality of motherhood for most of the world's women, in which they bear children against their will, are unable to provide basic necessities for their children, and are powerless to protect them from danger and abuse. The implicit biological determinism of this view obscures the value of women's choice in whether and when to become a mother. The use of this image to the exclusion of others fails to recognize that all women, whether they are mothers or not, exercise their physical, emotional, and intellectual powers in the world in varied ways. Mary Collins observes, "Women as women are also agents of justice and judgement; women act with fairness; women courageously use their power to challenge the mighty on behalf of the poor. . . . Are these not the characteristics of the one ineffable God YHWH in biblical tradition?"[48] However, in spite of the problems and risks associated with the use of the image of Mother for God, there are also good reasons not to reject it out of hand. The most significant of these is the necessity of reclaiming and revaluing the mothering experience of women. Although motherhood in the abstract is valued and romanticized in patriarchal culture, in reality it is devalued and ignored. Or to put it more bluntly, motherhood is valued; mothers (and children) are not. Popular culture, especially in the form of television shows and movies, routinely trivializes the work that mothers do, sentimentalizes the mother-child relationship, and at the same time blames mothers for their children's failures. When a woman in our culture chooses (supposing she has the choice) to become a mother, she is propelled, whether she chooses it or not, into this context. A God who can be called Mother must transcend this superficial cultural image of the mother to help us recognize the dangerous assumptions our culture carries about motherhood. Only thus can God as Mother serve as an important source of power and identity for women who are mothers.

Moreover, the image of God as Mother may, as the image of God as Father does, function in an extended metaphorical sense. In a study of Hindu Goddesses as a source for contemporary feminism, Rita Gross notes that even Goddesses who are called mother are not necessarily identified iconographically solely with giving birth. Rather, the term is used metaphorically:

> It seems that any act carried out by a female that produces positive results of some sort merits the title mother. This really should not be so hard to grasp, since we use language that way all the time in reference to God the Father, whom no one expects to be a cosmic universal inseminator. . . . Why then should God the Mother be an infinitely fertile birth-giver and caretaker of young children?[49]

We are familiar with this use of the term in Christian tradition for women who are mothers only in a metaphorical sense, such as Mother Teresa of Calcutta and other heads of religious communities. However, as Culpepper has noted, the use of motherhood as a metaphor for all kinds of creative activity may be too limiting, and easily slips into maternalism by implying that motherhood is somehow a superior form of creativity.

Taking a slightly different approach, Sallie McFague has proposed the use of the metaphor of God as Mother in order to speak not only of the birth-giving and creative aspects of God, but also of divine justice:

God as mother-creator is primarily involved not in the negative business of judging wayward individuals but in the positive business of creating with our help a just ecological economy for the well-being of all her creatures. God as the mother-judge is the one who establishes justice, not the one who hands out sentences.[50]

More significantly, however, McFague argues that the maternal metaphor for God must be only one among others, not the exclusive image. In this way, the mothering activity of many women may be recognized, but the dangers of stereotyping and limiting female images may be avoided.[51] Experientially, motherhood is a diverse phenomenon, and while some mothers may experience it as creative (at least in part), others may experience it as burdensome, frightening, and alienating. Only by allowing the image of God as Mother to be complex as well as one among other female images can this image be emancipatory for women.

GOD AS ONE

Monotheism is regarded as a basic theological principle of both Christianity and Judaism. Some feminists, however, are critical of the idea of monotheism as well as of its normative maleness. Emily Culpepper, as we already saw, is critical of Goddess monotheism as well. Arguing that the Goddess is a reductionist term, she says, "Any one concept inflated into The One God or The Goddess or The Right Way divides society into two groups: an elite that identifies with The One and an outcast group which the elite has had the power to stigmatize and define as Other, as evil, as less valued, even as sub- or non-human."[52] Similarly, Rita Gross has argued that monotheism tends to lead to hierarchical dualism, since diversity can only be accounted for as not part of the One, and thus of less value.[53] Such dualism has been historically very damaging for women in patriarchal religions such as Judaism and Christianity, wherein women are most unlike a male God and thus regarded as inferior and Other. However, as Culpepper reminds us, such monotheistic thinking even when the deity is female is also damaging to women, since a single female image cannot adequately include the diversity of women's lives, and easily lends itself to a divinization of women of the dominant social class (that is, white women) which makes women of color the Other.

But are pluralism and diversity always at odds with monotheism? Is there a way of recognizing the dangers of dualistic thinking implied in monotheism and intentionally avoiding them? Aside from the traditional value placed on monotheism within Christian and Jewish theology, is there feminist value in monotheism? It would seem that the feminist value that may be expressed by monotheism is the value of unity, also sometimes named solidarity or sisterhood. Although feminism is rightly suspicious about false or dichotomizing unity, which seeks to suppress difference and create separation, unity of spirit, which simultaneously recognizes and celebrates diversity and particularity, is an important value in the feminist movement. This kind of unity is seen as an antidote to the cultural emphasis on competition by valuing cooperation, and as a rejection of individualism by valuing relationships. It also makes it possible to emphasize the interconnection of all life on earth and to affirm the work of what Drorah Setel calls "repair of the world" as restoration of an essential unity.[54]

This feminist understanding of unity is clearly at odds with a narrow or superficial monotheism which has no room within it for diversity either in God or among the people supposedly created in the image of God. Nor can it be reconciled with a strict monotheism, which insists on absolute separation between God and nature. However, a monotheism that exists as unity-in-diversity and that permits reciprocity and cooperation is not only consistent with feminist concerns, but also potentially emancipatory. Drorah Setel argues that contemporary Judaism suffers from "a confusion between a belief in one God/dess and the belief in one *image* of God/dess."[55] She argues, therefore, that the one God/dess may be both unified and diverse, and translates the Jewish prayer which traditionally says "On that day the Lord shall be One and His Name shall be One," to say instead "On that day The-One-of-Being shall be unified and Her Names shall be infinite."[56]

GOD AS THREE-IN-ONE

Nothing has been more resistant to change than the traditional Christian language of the Trinity. Yet the foregoing discussion suggests that the idea of the "three-in-one" might be a very useful way of speaking of the kind of unity-in-diversity which we have just recommended. As traditionally used, of course, the language has been anything but helpful. At least in the dominant western Christian tradition the three persons of the Trinity have been spoken of as male. Only the relative vagueness of the third person of the Trinity, the Holy Spirit, has ever permitted the possibility of admitting female language into the Trinity. As Elizabeth Johnson has observed, however, when this has been proposed, it has usually been a way to reinforce cultural concepts of femininity rather than an attempt to include a female image of God in the Trinity.[57] Moreover, if only the third person of the Trinity can be spoken of as female, that still leaves the first and second firmly male. As Johnson notes:

> The overarching framework of this approach remains andro-centric, with the male principle still dominant and sovereign. The Spirit even as God remains the "third" person, easily subordinated to the other two, since she proceeds from them and is sent by them to mediate their presence and bring to completion what they have initiated.[58]

A second difficulty with traditional trinitarian language has been its tendency to use the relationship among the three persons of the trinity not to emphasize the relationship between God and humanity but to emphasize God's isolation from humanity and the rest of the created world.[59] This function of trinitarian language, what Sallie McFague calls "protecting God from any dependence on the world," may speak of communalism within God, but it is a communalism which is unrelated to the world, and thus it cannot answer the need for God-language that overcomes monistic dualism and celebrates diversity and relationship.

A third problem with traditional trinitarian language is its use as a liturgical test of orthodoxy. The most ancient use of trinitarian language in the liturgy, in the baptismal formulas and in the eucharistic prayer, is flexible and doxological rather than dogmatic or exclusionary. However, the frequent repetitions of the formula "Father, Son, and Holy Spirit", especially as it came to be attached to the ends of psalms, prayers, and hymns, came to serve as a kind of liturgical shibboleth to identify inadequate theology or at least to impose a kind of superficial doctrinal unity. Since women have routinely been defined by the church throughout its history as prototypical heretics, and since patriarchally defined doctrines have rarely been emancipatory for women, the alleged orthodoxy of trinitarian language and thought does not in itself suffice to recommend it from a feminist perspective.

All of these difficulties seem to spring from a common source similar to the one identified by Setel with respect to Jewish monotheism. That is, there is a confusion between belief in God as three-in-one on the one hand and belief that "Father, Son, and Holy Spirit" are the only names for God as three-in-one on the other. As McFague observes, there are many good reasons for using three as an image of God: it is dialectical; it is plural without being dualistic; it permits variety and richness.[60] But there is no need to assume that Father, Son, and Holy Spirit are the only ways to name this plural God. Again in McFague's words, "if it can be shown that models other than the traditional ones are appropriate and illuminating for expressing the Christian gospel in our time, an important admission will have been made: God has many names."[61]

Several attempts have been made to create alternative images for the Christian Trinity. The most familiar, arising from within the early feminist liturgical movement, is "Creator, Redeemer, Sustainer (or Sanctifier)." This practice has been criticized for substituting functional terms for relational, and indeed further feminist reflection on this formula suggests that relational terms are valuable from a feminist perspective.[62] A further difficulty with this formula, of course, is its lack of female images. As we discussed above, the elimination of male images alone is not emancipatory for women.

Gail Ramshaw-Schmidt suggests that in place of Father-Son-Spirit we use "Abba, Servant, Paraclete."[63] "In the naming of God," she argues, "Christians begin with the reality of Jesus." Therefore she structures her terminology by identifying Jesus as the Servant who suffers with us. From this starting point, then, Jesus' relationship to God determines the choice of "Abba" for the first person of the trinity: "Jesus' God is Abba, the loving parent, the gracious papa, the nurturing mother, the one who hears the cry of the servant. . . ."[64] The third person, the Paraclete, is the witness to both in the presence of the assembly as comforter, counselor, and advocate. Since the stated purpose of Ramshaw-Schmidt's proposal is inclusivity rather than emancipation, it is not surprising that there is no explicit female name offered in this formula. It has advantages over the "Creator, Redeemer, Sustainer" model by its use of biblical language and its somewhat more relational terminology. However, as Mary Collins has noted, the primacy which has been accorded the name Abba as a normative Christian name for God has been challenged by recent biblical scholarship, which has suggested not only that Jesus' use of Abba may not have been as unique as first thought, but also that other names, such as the I AM of John's Gospel, may be more normative, and equally biblical.[65] The insolubility of this sort of debate reveals the fundamental disability of approaches that attempt simply to "retranslate" the traditional trinitarian language without examining its basic assumptions.

Sallie McFague, in her book *Models of God*, has argued that the traditional trinitarian language has become absolutized, and proposes an imaginative, metaphorical approach in order not "to establish a new trinity using different names," but to "try out different models and metaphors," and offers the models of God as mother, lover, and friend.[66] Particularly important for our purposes, she insists that as part of this approach we must imagine God in female models as well as male, in order fully to express the *imago dei*. She makes two points about this: "First, God should be imagined in female, not feminine terms, and second, the female metaphors should be inclusive of but not limited to maternal ones."[67] In relation to the first point, she insists that the use of female pronouns is necessary in order to resist the temptation to stereotype. Nor can we skirt the issue by avoiding the use of pronouns for God altogether: "If we refuse to use any pronouns for God, we court the possibility of concealing androcentric assumptions behind abstractions."[68] In relation to her second point, she argues that her decision to focus on mother as a way of balancing the traditional image of father is not stereotyping, since she also speaks of creation and justice in female form. However, the risks of using the mother image as a model as Culpepper has identified them are reflected in McFague's proposal: "mothering is a female activity, . . . to give birth and to feed the young is simply what females do. . . ."[69] But this statement is not true. Some women are mothers, some are not. Even those women who are mothers are not *only* mothers, but also sisters, friends, lovers, workers. By using the model of mother as the only explicitly female model for God, McFague tends to absolutize mothering in a way that unfortunately is profoundly inadequate for women's experience and, in the long run, a limiting rather than emancipatory model. Even her images of God as creator and judge are subsumed under the umbrella of mothering, designated as *mother-creator* and *mother-judge*.

Another disadvantage to her choice of mother as the female model for God relates to her argument that sexuality is a valuable and too much neglected model for God's activity in the world. By using explicitly female language, we see that personal God-language is always sexual, since human beings are sexual beings. However, by limiting herself to mother as the female model for God, she connects female sexuality with motherhood in a way that fails to do justice to women's sexuality. Ancient Goddess religions tended to distinguish between the aspect of the Goddess that represented sexual pleasure and the aspect that represented fertility. Although this distinction undoubtedly has its roots in a lack of awareness about the causal relationship between sexual activity and reproduction, in contemporary experience these two activities are still separable, practically speaking. By relating, even implicitly, female sexuality and motherhood, the importance of women's choice about whether or not to bear a child is obscured and devalued.

This could have been avoided, for example, by using female pronouns in speaking of God as lover. Women's sexuality has been and still continues to be regarded in our culture as shameful and dangerous. By explicitly including female sexuality in a model of God which recognizes sexuality as a valuable model for God's activity in the world, women's sexual experience can be celebrated and delighted in. This model would take us a long way toward emancipating women from fear and hatred of our own bodies.

Similarly, McFague's model of God as friend also has powerful emancipatory potential for women, if it is made explicitly female by the use of female pronouns. Women's friendships have also been devalued and ridiculed, or looked upon with suspicion in our culture. Indeed, the whole western tradition of thought about friendship has been deeply misogynistic, assuming that women are morally and spiritually incapable of forming friendships.[70] Women have been expected to put their relationships with men above their relationships with other women or even children. But women's relationships with men have not been defined as friendships, which occur between equals, but as a relationship between superior and subordinate. Women's egalitarian relationships with men as well as with other women can be celebrated by claiming God as female friend.

CONSTRUCTING EMANCIPATORY GOD-LANGUAGE

Having examined some of the most serious issues confronting the project of constructing female God-language and having looked briefly at some current proposals for change, we may now summarize our findings and enumerate some basic principles, which may guide our efforts.

111

1. *Emancipatory God-language must challenge our colonized imaginations.* We must free ourselves to explore metaphors and models for Goddess in ways that allow the images to remain flexible and tensive, and prevent their hardening into idols.

2. *Emancipatory God-language must include explicitly female referents.* This means that we need to discover new female names for God, including Goddess, Mother, Sister, Lady, Queen, Grandmother. But it also means we need to use female pronouns freely to claim "neutral" names for God as female which can challenge androcentric assumptions, names such as Redeemer, Lover, Liberator, Friend, Judge.

3. *Emancipatory God-language must balance diversity and unity.* Because our inherited images of God have emphasized unity at the expense of diversity, it may be necessary at first to rediscover the values of diversity of models for God before we can place equal emphasis on the value of unity. However, diversity-in-unity is a useful guiding image for this process. This principle is particularly critical for the construction of female God-language, since we need to permit ourselves to recognize and claim as good the rich diversity of women's lives. An emphasis on diversity is also critical in preventing the absolutizing of any one female image over others.

4. *Female language for Goddess must be chosen and used with a critical eye toward its meaning and use in patriarchal religion and culture.* Some models, such as mother and perhaps lady, are so laden with patriarchal interpretation that they can function in an emancipatory way for women only if they have been critically redefined and carefully contextualized. Mother in particular can function as an emancipatory model for Goddess only if it is allowed to be one among others and used in such a way that challenges rather than reinforces patriarchal definitions of motherhood.

5. *A valuable resource for enlarging our imaginations about God-language is to be found in the varied and rich traditions of Goddess-worship, as practiced in ancient times, as continuing in the present, and as reconstructed by contemporary feminists.* Such a process of appropriation must be guided by respectful openness to the tradition and a willingness to experience it on

its own terms, as well as a critical study of its images, attending in particular to "sympathetic critics." For example, existing traditions such as the Yoruba celebrate Oshun the Dancer, and Yemaya of the seas, who give to humanity *ashe*, the power-to-make-things-happen.[71] The Laguna Pueblos revere Spider-Woman as the primordial diety, who gave fire to humankind.[72] Or perhaps the contemporary interpretation of the Triple Goddess can inform the Christian trinitarian model. The Virgin or Nymph aspect of the Goddess celebrates sexual pleasure and delight, corresponding perhaps to McFague's lover model. The second aspect is the mother, or preserver and protector of life, parallel in some ways to the traditional first person of the Trinity, or to McFague's mother model. The third aspect of the Goddess is the crone, or old woman, representing wisdom and death as part of life. Although both Christianity and Judaism have within their tradition an image of Wisdom as a female aspect of God, she is rarely presented as an aged woman. The devaluation of old women in our culture as well as our denial of the reality and finality of death makes the image of God as Old Woman a particularly powerful and significant one which deserves further exploration.[73]

6. *Emancipatory God-language must be firmly grounded in the lived experiences of real women, resisting romanticization and generalization.* As has been emphasized, women's experiences in a patriarchal society and church are often reason to lament, and metaphors for God drawn from women's experience may reveal God as the one who suffers and struggles for her own survival and for the survival of those who depend on her for their survival. They may reveal God as the one who cries out for justice. They may reveal Goddess as the one who is powerless in the face of injustice. Female metaphors for God will also have to take women's physical lives seriously, but also carefully guarding against romanticization of women's bodies. Metaphors that image God as having a female body may reveal her as one who enables women to love and respect their own and other women's bodies. Such metaphors may also reveal God as one whose body is violated and abused by those who are supposed to love her, or they may reveal God as one who

refuses to be violated, who resists her abuse, and who seeks justice against her abusers.

7. *Emancipatory God-language must also take into account the particularity of women's experience: the racial, ethnic, religious, and class distinctions, which divide us from one another as women, but which also make us distinctive.* Metaphors for God must be constructed not only on the basis of white western women's experiences, but must recognize the diversity of women's experiences in the present and in the past. Lest the construction of female God-language lead to the creation of a White Goddess, the experiences of women of color must contribute to the construction of new metaphors for God.

EMANCIPATORY LITURGICAL LANGUAGE

All such theorizing, analyzing, and deriving of principles must finally come to ground, however, in the liturgical assembly. There our speech is not only about God but also with God. The dialogue that takes place there is premised, as Mary Collins notes, not on the incomprehensibility of God but on her gracious self-disclosure.[74] The context is one not of critical inquiry but of faith. This premise has sometimes led theologians, and liturgical theologians in particular, to claim too much for that self-disclosure. For not all is disclosed, and we do well to remind ourselves of the fact that according to our own religious tradition the only divine name that has been revealed to us is both unpronounceable and untranslatable.

In fact, all liturgical language is necessarily metaphorical and contingent, and our language about the one who calls us into liturgical assembly is even more so. Gail Ramshaw-Schmidt describes this character of liturgical language well as a process of "yes-no-yes," wherein we recognize the revelation which comes to us in human language, we test and question and reform it, recognizing its profound limitations, and we finally acknowledge that in spite of its limitations, human language is the only way we have of speaking of the One whom we encounter in the assembly.[75]

However, when we allow ourselves to assume that this encounter with the living God is anything less than transformative, we have allowed our language to limit our relationship. Certainly the shift from God to Goddess, from he to she, is going to be perceived as a seismic one. It changes everything.

Some may be driven into silence by this seismic experience, not knowing how to speak. But silence has a long and honored place in all religious traditions as a means of communication with the One who is beyond all names and all human language. Silence before God can create the space necessary for new names, new models, and new images to begin to be recognizable, and can allow us to engage both our memories and our imaginations. Even a God who is nameless has that namelessness in common with countless women of past and present. Silence is also an acknowledgment that no names are sufficient, not only because the one we worship is beyond all human naming but also because even the power of human naming cannot restore to us what has already been lost through false naming. In describing her encounter with the female deity, "she of the several faces," Adrienne Rich, in the poem from which this chapter takes its title, says

I wished to cry loose my soul
   into her, to become
      free of speech at last.[76]

CHAPTER FIVE

"I AM WORD, SPIRIT, AND POWER"

The Bible and Emancipatory Preaching

We have observed in chapter 1 that the restoration of *biblical* liturgy has been an important goal of the liturgical movement. In this context *biblical* has meant two things. First, the reformed liturgies have attempted to claim biblical language and images as foundational for the liturgy. This is accomplished not by quotations of isolated verses but by the allusive and poetic use of terms, phrases, and images that link actions of the community to the events of the biblical tradition by the use of biblical typology. Second, the creation of new lectionary systems, especially those based on the three-year Roman Lectionary, has dramatically increased and broadened the amount of Bible read in the liturgy. This emphasis on the Bible in the liturgy serves at least two purposes: it corrects some of the late medieval and reformation confusions that had afflicted the liturgy, and it provides a place for ecumenical consensus. This recovery of the biblical character of the liturgy has gone hand in hand with a renewed interest in biblical preaching, especially preaching from the lectionary.

At the same time, feminist biblical scholars have advanced serious critiques of traditional interpretations of the Bible, challenging the uncritical use of biblical texts as well as methodologies that have rendered women in the biblical text invisible or marginal.[1] This critique recognizes that the biblical texts are androcentric in perspective and patriarchal in purpose. Differences among feminist interpreters arise from the different answers given to the question of the authority of Scripture. For post-Christian and post-Jewish feminists, the Bible itself is viewed as being much of the source of patriarchalism, and none of the solution. Thus the rejection of the Bible as authoritative is an essential part of this rejection of biblical religions. But even Christian feminists approach the Bible with a high degree of ambivalence, recognizing on the one hand that it should indeed bear a label, as Elisabeth Schüssler Fiorenza argues, saying, "Warning! Dangerous to women's health and survival," and knowing, on the other hand, that at least some of our experience of liberation can be traced to encounters with the biblical message.[2] This ambivalent attitude is caught well in a phrase of Letty Russell's: the "liberating word" and "liberating the word".[3] Women encounter the biblical call to liberation as a call addressed to us as women. At the same time, indeed as part of this call to liberation, comes the realization that the Bible itself is in need of liberation from its patriarchal context.

A similar ambivalence is reflected in Christian feminists' attitude toward preaching. Women have been and in some traditions continue to be denied access to the church's preaching office. It is little wonder that we wish to begin to speak for ourselves from the pulpit. Moreover, the silencing and subordination of women has frequently been proclaimed to us from the pulpit. The use of the preaching office as a means of domination and maintenance of clergy privilege is familiar to us, and thus our desire for access to the pulpit is always tempered by an awareness of its potential for authoritarianism and oppression.

There would seem to be very little common ground between these two movements on the subject of the authority of the Bible and the place of preaching in liturgy. Nevertheless, some common ground exists, however small it appears at first glance, in the search of both movements for tradition, or memory. The question that must be answered, however, is whether the Bible offers sufficient resources for the reconstruction of women's memory, and therefore whether a biblical liturgical tradition is sufficient. Also of concern to both movements is the interpretation of the biblical tradition, but here as well an uncritical approach to biblical preaching is open to feminist challenge.

We will take up these questions in turn, looking first at the question of the place and authority of the Bible in the liturgy, both as a source for guiding images and language, and as found in the public reading of Scripture. Then we will turn to the question of preaching and the possibilities of an emancipatory mode of preaching.

THE BIBLE IN LITURGY

The restoration of the use of biblical phrases, terms, and images to the liturgy is understood as a return to the practice of the ancient church. The typological use of Scripture in liturgy was common during the patristic era, particularly in the use of the Hebrew scriptures and in the search for parallels between Old and New Testaments. It would not be too great an exaggeration to say that much of the content of the change instituted by the liturgical movement has been a recovery of biblical typologies and the ability to think typologically.[4]

Typology is essentially simply the recognition of certain patterns within history that are repeated and are expected to recur. Thus "God saves through water" is a pattern that is recognized in the story of Noah, in the crossing of the Red Sea and the Jordan, in the baptism of Jesus in the Jordan, in the baptism of Christians in water. Within the pattern, furthermore, there are metaphors which allow the pattern to be interpreted in a variety of ways. Thus water works metaphorically as an allusion to death, life, birth, cleansing, and destruction.

This is particularly evident in the restoration of the Paschal Vigil in the reformed liturgies. In place of rites weakened by historicization or sentimentalism, the Great Vigil, in some reforms linked with the Triduum Sacrum, attempts to recall a liturgical appropriation of biblical events that is faithful to the historical nature of the events and also clearly connected to the gathered community. The Paschal Vigil, which includes as many as thirteen readings, recounts the history of God's relationship with God's people from the beginning of creation until the resurrection of Jesus Christ. Thus God's creation of the world is presented as a type of God's creative work, completed in the new creation brought about by the resurrection of Christ. God's salvation of Noah from the flood prefigures God's salvation of Christ from death; God's deliverance of the Israelites from the Egyptians at the Red Sea signals God's deliverance of Christ from the bonds of death, and so on. But these types do not operate only as biblical interpretation. They are explicitly connected to the gathered community by the communal ritual actions which follow the readings: baptism and eucharist. Thus God's creative and redemptive work continues in the liturgical life of the gathered community as God gives birth to new Christians reclaimed from death and nourishes the community at the messianic table.

Jean Daniélou defines typology as the "science of similitudes between the two Testaments."[5] Although, as Daniélou notes, typology was used by Jewish writers, especially the prophets, the use of typology by Christian writers, and especially in the liturgy, concerns us here. For in Christian usage this "science of similitudes" becomes a prophecy-fulfillment interpretation that forces all Hebrew (and other Jewish) scriptures into being prophecies of Jesus Christ. In this use, the patterns are not merely repeated, but progressive, so that the earlier patterns are seen to come to completion or fulfillment in later (that is, Christian) patterns. This method of interpretation has been under fire since the eighteenth century, first from the challenges of rationalism, later from the development of historical-critical interpretation of the Scriptures.[6] In this century, the recognition of the scandal of Christian anti-Semitism and the horror of the Holocaust make the simple acceptance of a naive prophecy-fulfillment interpretation of Scripture intolerable. Thus the attempt of the liturgical movement to restore a typological use of Scripture in liturgy appears to run counter to both historical-critical biblical studies and contemporary sensitivity to Jewish-Christian relations, quite aside from the feminist critique of the Bible.

A feminist critique of typological interpretation of Scripture would begin with a reiteration of the fundamental feminist critique of the Bible: It is a patriarchal and androcentric book, which has served and continues to serve the interests of men. The typological interpretation simply makes biblical events and persons into types that are unreflectively androcentric and patriarchal. A good example of this character of typology is the use of the figures of Adam and Eve, both of which have functioned as pivotal types for typological interpretation and for liturgy. Adam, a male, is used as a type of all of humanity, a type that is fulfilled in Jesus Christ, also a male. Eve, a female, is a type of sinful womanhood, or sometimes sinful humanity, a type which is fulfilled in Mary, whose passive obedience is emphasized against Eve's disobedience. Not only is such typology manifestly androcentric, it also serves, in the case of Mary, to obscure the historical woman behind the type.

Yet in spite of these serious problems with typology as an interpretive model, the use of it in reformed liturgies also answers some problems of contemporary worship. The most serious problem for the contemporary church is its relationship to its own history, especially its biblical history. The effect of rationalism on Christian worship has been a loss of imagination and therefore a loss of both the ability to experience awe and the ability to engage in ritual play. This rationalism has reduced worship to doctrinal instruction, moral instruction, or, in reaction to rationalism, a sentimental pietism. The ascendency of the historical-critical study of Scripture, although undeniably fruitful for the church's self-understanding on the whole, has also borne bitter fruit for the church's ability to worship. Where historical-critical scholarship has united with rationalism to claim an objective, value-free perspective, the cost to the liturgy has been great. For not only are such claims spurious, as feminist and other critics have pointed out, but they also make liturgical appropriation of Scripture highly problematic, since liturgy is neither objective nor value-free. Thus the role of Scripture in worship has been reduced to a source for doctrine or morality, or (again in reaction against historical criticism) to a "magical" book that is seen as entirely ahistorical.

The purpose of the liturgical movement's attempt to restore typological use of Scripture to the liturgy, then, is to overcome these problems, and to reestablish a lively sense of connectedness between the present gathered assembly for worship and the ancient scriptural texts. This connectedness is possible with a typological approach because it both recognizes the historical character of the scriptural text and simultaneously asserts that the historical event has a present claim on the worshiping community, and we on it. Only by claiming such a connectedness can history become memory for the liturgical community. However, as we have argued in previous chapters, this memory must include women and women's memories if it is not to be self-deceptive. What must a liturgical appropriation of Scripture do in order to connect both with ancient women of biblical religion and with contemporary women? Is a feminist typology possible?

A FEMINIST TYPOLOGY

It is possible, but only if typology is rather carefully defined. Typology, it must be noted, is not a method of interpretation exclusive to biblical interpreters. It is in fact a broadly human activity, native especially to poets in that it is analogical; it is a way of seeing that recognizes similarities between things that at first glance appear to have little in common. It is thereby revelatory, because this use of analogy enables the viewer to see connections not superficially apparent. Thus this kind of poetic seeing may also be eschatological and prophetic.[7] Since we have dealt with the importance of revelatory, poetic seeing in the construction of feminist liturgical tradition in previous chapters, we shall here deal only with the possibilities of this approach for the liturgical use of Scripture.

The best possibility for developing a feminist typological method for the liturgical use of Scripture lies in the fundamentally dialogical character of the method. The term *type* means simply a mold, pattern, or impression. The companion term, *antitype,* literally means an answer or response to the original pattern. Although in a polemical and anti-Jewish context these terms took on an adversarial connotation, such use of the terms is dictated not by the terms themselves, but by their users. The liturgical term similar to *antitype* is *antiphon,* an answering sound, a sung response which enters into dialogue with the biblical text. Thus while this meaning of the terms *type* and *antitype* is not that used by the ancient church, neither is this meaning alien to the terms themselves, especially in a liturgical context.

A feminist typology then must be dialogical; that is, it engages the Scriptures in dialogue. In the liturgy the scriptures are engaged in dialogue with themselves in a way that can recognize the diversity of the biblical witness about women. But also the gathered community is engaged in dialogue with the Scriptures, so that the ambivalence of the relationship between the community and the Scriptures can be fully acknowledged. Moreover, this dialogical character, if it is to be fully emancipatory, must intentionally resist the temptation to collapse the particularities of the participants in the dialogue: in this case, the Hebrew Scriptures, the Christian Scriptures, and the gathered community. This particularity demands that the poetic character of the biblical types, or patterns, that emerge must be recognized as such, and the temptation to make these patterns into immutable archetypes must also be resisted.

A second characteristic of typology that is relevant for the construction of feminist typology is the method by which types are generated, or discovered. Even in the biblical uses of typology, the user begins not with a scriptural text within which types are sought, but with a communal experience that demands understanding. Thus the Jewish people in exile sought understanding about their apparent abandonment by God, and found in the stories of God's deliverance hope for their own eventual deliverance. Thus the early Christians, attempting to understand the death and resurrection of Jesus, found stories of God's messianic promises that answered their need. Thus at times of great crisis, when the accepted reality is called into question, types serve as reassurance that there is continuity with one's own past as well as hope for the future.

Similarly the generation and discovery of feminist typology will be motivated not first of all by biblical research but by conscious appropriation of women's experiences of struggle against patriarchy in society and in the church. As women become aware of the patterns of oppression of women and others in patriarchy, we are able to discover the same patterns in biblical narrative. As we begin to recognize and name forms of resistance and strategies for survival, we are then in a position to identify the same forms in biblical stories. Thus these biblical types, so identified, can function to connect us with the biblical story and offer us hope in the knowledge that we do not struggle alone.

Such a process assumes that women have both the necessary knowledge of the Bible and the will to do such study. However, the Bible has functioned in such a destructive way for women for so many centuries that it is uncertain whether this process is feasible today. Women engaged in a process of recognizing and naming their oppression experience a profound sense of alienation from the Bible as the source of much of their oppression.

And yet such feminist typology has already begun to emerge as a result of feminist biblical interpretation, and more will continue to emerge as such scholarship continues and develops. This is not to suggest that types emerge directly from scholarship, but rather that committed feminist scholarship identifies important events and figures for women's memory, and that the importance of these typological events and persons is ratified by their influence on developing feminist liturgies.

This dialectical process is well exemplified, for example, in the evolution of a liturgy recorded in *Image Breaking, Image Building,* called "Search for the Lost Coin".[8] The liturgy is built around the pericope from Luke 15, in which a woman searches her house until she finds a coin that has been lost. The process

123

of searching is identified with women's search for something of value in a tradition that has devalued them. This interpretation is influenced by Phyllis Trible's use of the parable at the conclusion of *God and the Rhetoric of Sexuality,* wherein the woman's search for the coin is identified with Trible's search, in the book, for "the lost token of faith", in particular, positive female images.[9] Significantly, she notes the priority of feminist concerns which helped to shape her study.[10] Also significantly, the liturgy built around this text, although clearly indebted to Trible's use of the parable, also goes beyond it, by identifying the search as a broader one than the question of biblical interpretation and also by seeing in the coins, which were not really lost, a way of recognizing the positive values in the Christian tradition already experienced by women. Thus the story functions as a type of women's struggle to come to terms with their Christian tradition in a way that recognizes both the values that are present as well as the values that have been lost.

Examples may be multiplied, for example, the woman bent double of Luke 13 who is healed by Jesus in the synagogue and who "stood up straight and praised God," is a type of women's struggle for recognition in the church, especially ordination. Or the woman with the oil who anointed Jesus' head before his death, cited by Elisabeth Schüssler Fiorenza in the title of *In Memory of Her,* as a type of women's prophetic leadership in the tradition, as well as the tradition's neglect of women's stories. Or the community of women mourning each year for the death of Jephthah's daughter, cited by Phyllis Trible, which serves as a type of women's communities of worship and of the need to lament the unnecessary suffering and violence in women's lives under patriarchy.[11] All of these stories, and others, have influenced feminist liturgies. In each case, as well, it was experience with the contemporary struggles of women for emancipation that gave rise to the scholarly interpretations as well as the liturgical events.

Finally, feminist typology must, like traditional liturgical typology, be allowed to connect with the reality of the gathered community through the use of sacraments, especially the church's central sacraments of baptism and eucharist. Although the possibilities for feminist sacramental theology will be explored in the next chapter, it should be noted here that the sacramental experience of biblical types recognized in women's experiences of struggle and survival is a necessary component of feminist typlogy.

The use of feminist typologies has influenced the generation of feminist liturgies, but they have yet to influence in a significant way the reformed liturgies being produced within the various traditions. For them to do so, they would have to become part of the typological vocabulary of the liturgy and thus inform the language of prayer, liturgical year, and sacrament; they would have to become part of the lectionary cycle; and they would have to become part of the church's homiletical vocabulary.

FEMINIST TYPOLOGY AND THE LECTIONARY

Since the lectionary itself is shaped by the church year, feminist anamnesis must be allowed to influence the seasons and feasts of the yearly cycle. This is most fruitfully done by first recognizing the christological character of the two major cycles, focusing on the incarnation (Advent, Christmas, Epiphany), and on the death and resurrection of Christ (Lent, Easter, Pentecost), and then viewing each of these through women's eyes and from women's perspectives. A feminist emancipatory view of these events would need to take seriously the presence of women at these biblical events as well as in the gathered community.

Although the lectionary is shaped by the church year, the content of the lectionary readings, more than anything else, gives each season and feast its character. Thus the process of beginning to see the central constitutive events of Christianity through women's eyes can begin with the texts chosen for the lectionary. A critical examination of the texts of one widely used version of the three-year lectionary reveals that an androcentric hermeneutic has influenced both the choice of

125

texts to be included and the way in which the three readings and psalm for each Sunday are related to one another.[12] When women appear at all in the texts, it is as adjuncts to male actors, never as agents in their own right. The only exception to this rule are texts about marriage, which emphasize women's procreative role over men's, and which presume a patriarchal model of marriage. Even lectionary texts from the book of Ruth, which is only marginally about marriage, are interpreted as celebrating patriarchal marriage by using marriage psalms with the texts.[13] Where women are unequivocally present in the texts, such as at the crossing of the Red Sea by the Israelites, or at the crucifixion and empty tomb of Jesus, the lectionary makes presence into absence by omitting or making optional the verses which name or mention the women.[14]

The texts that are emerging as feminist typological texts, such as the woman searching for the lost coin, the woman who appointed Jesus' head before his death, the healing of the woman bent double, Jephtha's sacrificed daughter, the raped and murdered concubine, and so on, are notably absent from the lectionary. Without the presence of such texts, the evolution of feminist anamnesis is not possible. At the same time that these texts are absent, patriarchal texts demanding the silence and submission of women are still included without apology or contrast, as if no emancipatory biblical tradition existed to counter such tradition. Thus women's present attempts to free ourselves from patriarchy appear as if for the first time and as if such attempts are opposed by the revealed Word of God in Scripture.

A feminist lectionary must take seriously women's struggle for survival and dignity not only in the present but also in the biblical past. Thus texts that call forth lament as well as those which call forth celebration must be included. The presence of women at central constitutive events of the faith suggests one way to begin to claim and reconstruct women's memory for the church. The use of feminist typology offers a way to connect the struggles and joys of contemporary women of biblical religion with our past. As Elisabeth Schüssler Fiorenza puts it,

We participate in the same struggle as our biblical foresisters against the oppression of patriarchy and for survival and freedom from it. We share the same liberating visions and commitments as our biblical foremothers. We are not called to "empathize" or to "identify" with *their* struggles and hopes but to continue *our* struggle in solidarity with them. Their memory and remembrance—rediscovered and kept alive in historical reconstruction and actualized in ritual celebration—encourage us in historical solidarity with them to commit ourselves to the continuing struggle against patriarchy in society and church.[15]

FEMINIST EMANCIPATORY PREACHING

As was noted earlier in this chapter, feminists have been rightly critical of authoritarian modes of biblical interpretation from the pulpit. Yet as has already been suggested, it is an essential part of the reconstruction of women's liturgical tradition that women begin to break silence and speak aloud in public. If feminist emancipatory language in its verbal and nonverbal forms intends to make women visible, if feminist hermeneutics intends to make biblical women visible, and if feminist typology connects biblical tradition with contemporary women's struggles, then feminist preaching aims to make women audible.

Making women audible, enabling women to find our own voices and recognize and claim our right to speak is a fundamental necessity of the construction of feminist liturgical tradition and celebration. Women have been silenced by our own religious and cultural traditions, and this silencing has rendered us powerless. It has also distorted our traditions, making it appear as if women in fact had no voice, and therefore no ideas, no claims on the community, and no tradition or memory of our own. It has permitted others to speak for us, to tell us who we are, what we want and need, and what our past and future are. This can only begin to change when women claim the right to speak, and to speak out of our experience of struggle as women.

This speaking in our own voice is also critical to the

reconstruction of knowledge, especially our theological-liturgical knowledge. Researchers Mary Field Belenky, Blythe McVicker Clinchy, Nancy Rule Goldberger, and Jill Mattuck Tarule have studied the evolution of women's intellectual development.[16] The results of their study demonstrate the costs of this silence and denial of voice to women. On the basis of interviews with 135 women from a variety of educational settings, the authors identified five different modes or ways that the women acquired knowledge. Central to all of these was the struggle of women to find their own voice. Indeed, the first category they identified they named "silence." Women in this position "experience themselves as mindless and voiceless and subject to the whims of external authority."[17] Their family environment was typically characterized by a high degree of violence and abuse that was often used to enforce the women's silence. Moreover, in each category the major struggle was for the women to find their "voice," to discover some way to begin to speak, even when, as in the case of the "received knowers," the speaking only reproduced knowledge given by external authorities, and the primary posture was that of listening. As the authors themselves note, the metaphor of voice and silence arose from the women they interviewed:

> In describing their lives, women commonly talked about voice and silence: "speaking up," "speaking out," "being silenced," "not being heard," "really listening," "really talking," "words as weapons," "feeling deaf and dumb," "having no words," "saying what you mean," "listening to be heard" and so on in an endless variety of connotations having to do with a sense of mind, self-worth, and feelings of isolation from or connection to others. We found that women repeatedly used the metaphor of voice to depict their intellectual and moral development; and that the development of a sense of voice, mind, and self were intricately intertwined.[18]

Also as the authors observed, the women's process of gaining a voice was very often hampered by experiences of sexual abuse, frequently in childhood or adolescence. The authors note:

> In our sample of seventy-five women, 38 percent of the women in schools and colleges and 65 percent of women contacted through the social agencies told us that they had been subject to

either incest, rape, or sexual seduction by a male in authority over them—fathers, uncles, teachers, doctors, clerics, bosses. Abuse was not limited to any particular epistemological grouping of women in our study, nor was it limited to any specific class, ethnic, or age group.[19]

Of particular significance in these accounts of abuse is the imposition of silence on the victim by the abuser, often enforced with threats of physical violence. Thus breaking women's silence is an act of power that undercuts the power of the abuser, the power of the patriarchal society which permits such abuse, the power of the patriarchal church which refuses to recognize the abuse, sometimes inflicted by its own male clergy.

It could be argued that preaching is a patriarchal mode of action that is inevitably authoritarian and alienating and thus has no place in feminist liturgical experience. It is worth noting that Rosemary Radford Ruether makes no mention of preaching as one of the necessary functions of ministers in her discussion of ministry in women-church, although she does not explicitly exclude it either.[20] On the other hand, several books of women's sermons have been published in the past several years, and their contents attest to the importance that many women accord to women's preaching task in the church.[21]

Although preaching has certainly been used in an authoritative and alienating manner, it need not be either. It is a task that women need to claim in its emancipatory capacity. The authoritative, representative speaking involved in preaching is an act that can move us from silence into *having a voice* as women, both in the church and in the world. Such speaking has at least three implications for the church and its identity.

1. *Women are part of the world.* The silencing of women has made possible the androcentric ideology that men are normative human beings and women secondary and derivative. According to this ideology, men are in the world, but women only occupy a place within it. "Women's place" in the world is private, not public, peripheral, not central. It is not in

the world at all, in the sense that the term is usually used. When women break the imposed silence, this ideology can no longer stand, for our speaking the truth of our lives calls our marginalization into question. Moreover, speaking from the pulpit is a potent form of public speech, a particular kind of speaking women are not supposed to do. In androcentric ideology, women cannot be public figures, since we are defined as secondary and derivative. When we preach publicly, we take on the activity of a public person. This action not only shatters the notion of *women's place,* but also radically challenges the notion of what constitutes *the world.*

2. *Women are part of the church.* While women normally constitute the overwhelming majority of church members, our silencing has made us oddly invisible. Our role in the church, like that in society, has been defined for us as being similarly peripheral and private. This definition has made it possible for the churches to exploit our labor by claiming that it is our "nature" to work behind the scenes and that it is un-Christian to desire recognition or payment for our work. But when we break the silence by preaching, we openly challenge the assumption that our work is insignificant or peripheral. We claim that women can represent the church and humanity as fully as men do. We demonstrate that God can speak to a gathered community through a woman, with a woman's voice.

3. *Women bring women's experiences of struggle and survival in a patriarchal church and culture to the task of preaching.* The content of women's preaching is distinctive not because of biological determinism, but because we occupy a different place than men in society and in the church. This is not to claim that the experience of oppression or suffering gives women a position of moral superiority, but rather that our experience, when consciously reflected upon, gives us a distinctive perspective from which to view the Scriptures, the church, and the world. It is also to claim again the significance of particularity for our theological work, and in this case, for the work of preaching. In order to preach with authority, we must speak out of the particularity of our own experiences as women. This means

being able to recognize and name the patterns and forms of oppression we experience and observe. It means learning to identify the strategies for survival and possibilities for change that women have used in the past and continue to use in the present. This identification of types, discussed above in connection with interpretation of scripture, also can shape the way we preach. The result of this process will be to bring into the preaching event stories that have not been regarded as appropriate homiletical material: stories of women's poverty and hunger, of inadequate or abusive health care, of pornography and sexual violence, of rape and the threat of rape, of denial of control over our own bodies. It is essential that such stories become the subject of Christian preaching, however, because for millions of women some or all of these abuses are a daily reality. For all women in patriarchal society, abuse is always a possibility. To maintain silence in the face of such reality is to be complicit in its perpetuation. Feminist emancipatory preaching, in order to be responsible to women, speaks up about women's experience, and it does so in a context of proclamation of the gospel.

PREACHING AND LANGUAGE

In chapter 3 we argued that we need to develop emancipatory language in both verbal and nonverbal ways. Relative to preaching, this demands application of models of honest and imaginative language and reciprocal body language to the homiletical task.

The body language normally associated with preaching is marked by the use of symbols and gestures of dominance. The use of official, sacred space, physical elevation, both by the pulpit and by the preacher's standing while other sit, the use of special clothing or other signs of office (such as preaching stoles), and one-way speaking typically characterize preaching in most churches. Common assumptions about preaching include the identification of the sermon as the word of God and the conviction that the sermon is for the most part above criticism, an assumption reinforced by the monological character of most sermons. In particular, biblical sermons claim continuity with and the authority of the word of God by their placement within the service and by connection to the content of the Scripture reading. And the reading of Scripture itself is also surrounded by gestures of dominance, including restricting access to the book to ordained or otherwise authorized persons; introducing the reading with processions, acclamations, and bows; announcing and concluding the reading as "the Word of God"; reading from an elevated or restricted space.

Emancipatory preaching must discover gestures that establish and reinforce not dominance and submission but mutuality between preacher and community. The arrangement of space for speaking and hearing must allow for both audibility and reciprocity. The community may be encouraged in part by the space itself to see themselves as part of the proclamatory event and enabled to participate in the event by responding verbally to the sermon either in the course of or immediately following the sermon. The preacher may choose to stand, to sit, or to move around while delivering the sermon, but the choice will be made or at least principally based on the community's need to be engaged in the process of preaching. The authority of the sermon depends not on the use of traditional symbols and gestures of dominance, but on the authenticity of what is preached, and its accountability to women.

This then is the primary mark of feminist emancipatory preaching: this sense of accountability to women and women's struggles against patriarchy in the church and in society. Such preaching may take any of a variety of forms or use any one of a number of methods. Feminist emancipatory preaching may be at various times expository, doctrinal, biblical, narrative, poetic, or dramatic. But regardless of the form, feminist emancipatory preaching grows out of a consciousness of and commitment to women's struggle for emancipation. This commitment to change, joined with feminist interpretation of scripture and use of feminist emancipatory language, makes feminist emancipatory preaching possible.

Second, feminist emancipatory preaching is grounded in experiences of working for change for women in church and society. Preaching from women's experience without also engaging oneself in women's struggle for emancipation runs the risk of further exploiting women's oppression. This is particularly a danger for women who are privileged enough to have access to preaching (and therefore have acquired some degree of higher education and church authorization). We must not only remember and speak of the women who are silenced by lack of privilege, but we must work to empower them to speak, rather than let them become sermon illustrations.

This leads to the third mark of feminist preaching: it is dialogical, communal, and participatory. This does not necessarily mean that it must be a "dialogue sermon" in the literal sense, or that dialogue must always take place in the context of the delivery of the sermon itself, although it might. More generally, however, it means that the conception and construction of the sermon is understood as belonging to the community, in particular the community of women. It means that the preacher conceives and offers the sermon with the most silenced women in mind, hearing it through their ears, seeing it through their eyes.[22] A model of this sense of dialogue can be grasped from Nikki Giovanni's description of the origins and purpose of the "call-and-response" character of black preaching and music:

> Just imagine what a slave ship must have sounded like to a woman. The humming must have been deafening. It had to be there. The hum, the gospel, the call-and-response came over because it's here. The men didn't bring it over. . . . They didn't bring the field hollers because they didn't know them. They were not field men. They were hunters. Hunters don't make noise. So what we're hearing in the music is the women. . . . We were communal even then, and as we got into bigger fields, we would call to one another. If you didn't answer back, we went to see about you. . . . So what you're hearing in our music is nothing but the sound of a woman calling another woman.[23]

The feminist emancipatory sermon, marked by a sense of accountability to women and growing out of continuing dialogue with other women, must have "the sound of a woman calling another woman."

The fourth mark of feminist emancipatory preaching is related to this. The purpose of the sermon is to empower women. It speaks up and speaks out for women not only out of a sense of responsibility to women, and not only after engagement in work to change women's status in church and society, but also as part of that process of change. The feminist emancipatory sermon seeks to speak up for women only in order to empower all women to speak up and out for ourselves. Thus it may be that in a truly and fully emancipated church, in a fully emancipated world, in which women are no longer silenced, preaching will not be necessary. Until such time, however, feminist emancipatory preaching, among other forms of emancipatory speech, is necessary for our salvation.

Finally, feminist emancipatory preaching is biblical in the sense that it claims from Scripture the authority of women to speak and act on our own behalf, and it finds in Scripture not only the story of our silencing and oppression as women, but also the story of our struggle against oppression, our claim to power, and the source of our hope for the future. For this task of feminist preaching, we depend on the work of feminist biblical scholars who help us identify these sources of our own past and our hope for the future.

A fundamental assumption of the construction of feminist typologies and lectionaries, and the possibility of feminist emancipatory preaching, is that women in the church have the power and the authority to interpret the Bible. Although this may seem to be a radical claim, one that calls into question the traditional assumptions about the authority of Scripture, it in fact has long precedence in traditions of biblical religions. Of course, one may point out that men have always assumed the right to do this: to choose some scriptures and to reject others; to interpret Scripture texts according to the perceived needs of the occasion; to speak for God and to interpret God's word for others. More significantly, however, feminist biblical scholarship has revealed to us the ways in which women also have been involved in this process, sometimes with the approval of the male religious structure, sometimes not. So Huldah interpreted the word of God for Josiah and the people of Israel, and confirmed the authenticity of the book of the law. So women took leadership in the Jewish synagogues and read and interpreted the law to the people.[24] So women in the early Christian missionary movement preached the gospel. So the early Christian Montanist prophet Maximilla, claiming her authority in the face of persecution, declared, "I am chased like a wolf from the flock of sheep; I am not a wolf: I am Word, and Spirit, and Power."[25]

CHAPTER SIX

"WE MUST LEARN OUR COMMON SYMBOLS"

Baptism and Eucharist

Any religious movement dedicated to transformation must examine carefully its central constitutive rites. For Christianity this means baptism and eucharist: the rite of initiation and the rite of ongoing nurture. In these rites—their actions, objects, and words—the character of the Christian community is expressed and maintained. Moreover, by means of these rites the divine presence is believed to be mediated to the community in a privileged way. The liturgical movement has brought about significant reform of baptismal and eucharistic practice and faith. If the feminist liturgical movement is to transform Christianity at its heart, it too must affect sacramental practice by offering feminist critique of these rites as practiced by Christian communities and by bringing about change where it is called for.

Any feminist discussion of the sacraments, however, must begin with the acknowledgment of a deep sense of ambivalence. Although women's experience of baptism and eucharist has been at times an important source of power and strength to women in their struggle for dignity and survival, at other times sacramental events have been occasions of profound alienation. As Elizabeth Carroll notes, "By admitting women to Baptism the early Church acknowledged the full potentiality of the female to live the new life of the risen Christ, to receive and be driven by the charisms of the Holy Spirit, and to fulfill the promise of their Creator as imaging God."[1] Authority for this understanding of baptism is found in Galatians 3:27-28: "For as many of you as were baptized into Christ have put on Christ. There is neither Jew nor Greek, there is neither slave nor free, there is neither male nor female; for you are all one in Christ Jesus."[2] At the same time, this equality is experienced as being frequently thwarted by the church itself, especially in the celebration of the sacraments and the restriction of women's access to them. Helen Wright observes, "For more and more women, the Eucharistic celebration is becoming an experience of segregation and alienation."[3]

Fundamentally this is not so much a critique of the sacraments themselves as a critique of the patriarchal nature of the ecclesial context in which they occur.[4] If one understands the sacraments as acts that constitute or bring into being and sustain the church, however, the critique has serious implications for sacramental theology and practice. By beginning with a recognition of the social and political context within which the sacraments are celebrated, we follow the approach taken by liberation theologians, who have interpreted the liturgy and especially the eucharist as politically and socially oppressive in particular social contexts.[5]

FEMINIST CRITIQUE OF BAPTISM AND EUCHARIST

A feminist critique of Christian sacraments to some extent parallels the feminist critique of Christian symbols generally, since the sacraments are in a sense enacted symbols, or better, complexes of symbols. This critique may be summed up as follows: These enacted symbols function within a patriarchal and androcentric context and serve to reinforce men's power and deny women's power. More particularly, in the case of the sacraments, it is male clerical power that is reinforced and protected. The long history of denial of clerical power to women (and its continuation among the majority of the world's Christians) is focused with particular sharpness in the enactment of the sacraments. Thus the clericalization of the sacraments serves to protect male privilege in the church, and to deny power to women, as well as to render the laity passive.

To be more precise, the sacraments have traditionally functioned to legitimate male power (by restricting sacramental or consecratory power to men), to value men's bodies as being more "like Christ" than women's (by denying or limiting women's access to ordination), to value men's will and initiative over women's (by giving men control over not only the sacraments themselves but also access to the sacraments), and to sacralize men's bonds and heritage (especially through a male celibate priesthood, but also more subtly in defining sacramental ministry as a male vocation to which women can be admitted only under carefully controlled circumstances).

Moreover, the rites themselves, because they are rites of initiation and sustenance, serve to initiate both women and men into a patriarchal ecclesial structure and to maintain their identity with that structure even when it is oppressive. Thus the rites of baptism and eucharist, as enacted in a patriarchal church, both construct and sustain the patriarchal structure of church. This raises for women the serious question of their participation in rites that create and sustain a church that is not only clerical, hierarchical, and oppressive, but also misogynist and therefore particularly destructive for women. Therefore the fundamental question for feminists has not been how to reform the sacraments but how to transform the church to make it not only safe but empowering for women. However, the creating and sustaining functions of the sacraments should not be overlooked, since radically restructured rites of initiation and sustenance could construct a different institution.

At this point we must give serious consideration to the model of women-church, which has been developed by feminist communities of prayer and ritual as one possible response to this dilemma faced by Christian feminists. The development of such worshiping communities of women has been motivated by several factors: a growing dissatisfaction with the intolerance of many communities for feminist thought or practice; an awareness of the need for feminist theology to be more than ideas, and a desire to put the ideas into practice in a way usually disallowed in Christian communities; the need for a "free space" for Christian feminists to experiment with developing their own liturgies and rituals.[6] By naming these communities "women-church," these groups make an important claim for themselves and for the church. Namely, they are claiming that they are not schismatic, but intend to remain within the church; they also "claim the center," as Elisabeth Schüssler Fiorenza terms it, by refusing to be marginalized and by insisting that women are the church. By so doing, these communities are able to claim for themselves the freedom to act on their own behalf rather than wait on the decisions of male church leaders. Schüssler Fiorenza sums up the work of women-church as follows:

> As the church of women we celebrate our religious powers and ritualize our visions for change and liberation. We bond together in struggling with all women for liberation, and we share our strength in nurturing each other in the full awareness and recognition that the church of women is always the *ecclesia reformanda*, the church on the way to and in need of conversion and "revolutionary patience," patience with our own failures as well as with those of our sisters.[7]

As both Schüssler Fiorenza and Ruether make clear, women-church is not a separatist movement. Ruether describes it as an "exodus community" on a journey "out of patriarchy," while Schüssler Fiorenza sees it as a local manifestation of the vision of the universal church.[8] Moreover, as both theologians insist, it is not a new idea or movement, but one which, as Ruether says, may be "as old as the idea of Church itself as an exodus community against structures of oppression. Wherever the liberating Church implied that its exodus included women (and it has always implied this), and women themselves identified with it as subjects of their own humanity (as they have, again and again), the seeds of women-church were present."[9] Rather than being separatist, women-church moves intentionally toward mutuality, conscious that mutuality between women and men in the church can exist only as both women and men challenge the oppressive structures of patriarchy and engage in the work of liberating all oppressed people.[10]

The sacramental implications of the existence of women-church are two: first, women-church is church, and therefore claims rights for itself "by claiming our own spiritual powers and gifts, by deciding our own welfare, [and] by standing accountable for our decisions."[11] This includes the right to interpret and reform sacramental practice so that the sacraments build up an emancipatory church rather than a patriarchal one. Second, the women-church movement is part of the church universal, and therefore is able to benefit from the accumulated wisdom and insight of other movements within the church, especially those, such as the liturgical movement, dedicated to reform and transformation.

BAPTISM AND EUCHARIST IN THE LITURGICAL MOVEMENT

An important consequence of the liturgical movement for sacramental theology has been the shift of scholarly focus from dogmatic and legalistic controversies to the shape and content of the rites themselves. In the case of baptism and eucharist especially this has had a salutary ecumenical effect. There are scarcely any other religious practices that have been more divisive for Christians. Yet historical and theological reconstruction of ancient rites has made evident the commonality of our heritage as well as the polemical and contingent nature of many of the old controversies. Consequently, even the casual observer can hardly fail to be struck by the similarities among contemporary reformed rites of baptism and eucharist as developed by Christians with divergent and even historically opposed traditions. Although there is growing ecumenical consensus for other rites and sacraments, such as marriage rites, ordination rites, and daily prayer, the evolution of these rites has waited upon the relative consensus of these two central constitutive rites of Christianity.

The effects of the liturgical movement on baptismal and eucharistic practice and faith in the contemporary church have been many and far reaching. Although there are notable differences to be discerned among the different Christian traditions, the influence of the ecumenical liturgical movement can be seen in the recognizable common threads. These common threads, these ecumenical emphases, concern us here. We may discern four of these emphases that have deeply influenced liturgical reform and also provide a context from which to examine a feminist critique of Christian sacramental practice. These four are: (1) a recovery of historical perspective on sacramental practice and faith, (2) a renewed appropriation of typology, (3) a revaluation of the nonverbal elements of sacramental rites, and (4) an explicit articulation of justice issues implicit in the sacraments.

The historical recovery of early baptismal and eucharistic practices has, by attending less to dogmatic concerns and more to the actions and shape of the rites themselves, revealed the narrowness of the medieval concerns that we have all inherited and has opened up possibilities for fresh appropriation and interpretation of these practices. For example, historical research has shown us the disintegration of the rites of initiation from a complex and dramatic series of events to the marginal, desiccated rites familiar to most Protestants and Catholics today. Narrow and devalued understandings of baptism, as either a semi-magical removal of the stain of original sin or as nothing more serious than a naming ceremony for an infant, have gradually begun to give way before a reclamation of the richness of the early church's understanding of baptism as a multivalent symbol, representing rebirth, death and resurrection, messianic anointing, incorporation into a priestly people, to name but a few. The ancient church's apparent comfort with a variety of interpretations of their sacramental rites challenges our post-Reformation and post-Enlightenment tendency to restrict interpretations and search for the "correct" one.

Similarly, the study of early eucharistic practice has recovered, among other things, the connection between Christian eucharistic praying and Jewish praying, and has expanded the focus on a penitential remembrance of Jesus' death to include grateful thanksgiving for his resurrection. As

141

with baptism, the multivalence of the eucharistic action as understood by the ancient church has challenged us to rethink our interpretations of the meaning of Christ's presence and sacrifice as embodied in the eucharistic action, as well as reclaiming forgotten associations, such as feast of liberation and messianic banquet. These changes in historical perspective are in evidence in all the reformed rites, in the creation of baptismal rites that recover some of the richness of images and the drama of early practice, and in the restoration of the eucharist to the normative Sunday service for Protestants and the creation of new eucharistic prayers that reflect a wider range of interpretations of the event.

This sharpened historical perspective has also revealed the extent to which the rites of the early Christians were shaped by a typological appropriation of the Jewish Scriptures (which of course were also their own). In this sense especially, the reformed rites have claimed to be *biblical*. They refer to biblical events in a symbolic and poetic way so as to reveal the significance of the rite, its relationship to the community's past, and its claim on the present gathered community. So, for example, the baptismal rite may refer to God moving over the face of the deep at creation; God's destruction of the world by water and God's salvation of Noah's family from water by water; the liberation of the Israelites at the crossing of the Red Sea; the Israelites' crossing of the Jordan into the promised land; the baptism of Jesus in the Jordan, and so on. By piling up these varied images of God's working through water, by their implicit association with experiences of death, life, and liberation, of promises made and promises fulfilled, the act of baptism, which occurs within a particular community involving particular individuals is revealed in its larger context, and something of its significance is manifested. Similarly, the revised eucharistic rites evoke not only the last supper or the crucifixion but God's creative and redemptive activity from creation through the prophets, Jesus' meals with his disciples (both pre- and post-resurrection), and the promised eschatological feast.[12] By recalling God's ongoing care and faithfulness, the community gathered around the eucharistic table is assured of God's care for this particular community at this particular time and place.

Just as the renewed use of biblical typology has attempted to connect the gathered community with its own heritage, so the revaluation of gesture, movement, and objects or elements has moved to make the sacraments more dramatic and more immediate. The use of plenty of water in baptism and of real bread and wine in the eucharistic meal are intended in part to remind the community of the mundane origins of these rites in bath and in meal. But at the same time that the ordinariness of the elements used is emphasized, there is also a desire to communicate the sacred character of the event through the use of gesture and art. Indeed in the very simplicity of the elements, of water and oil, bread and wine, is seen evidence of God's gracious presence in and love for the world; and vesture, movement, and art direct the community's attention to the revelatory character of these elements.[13]

Finally, there is, at least on the part of some, an interest in the justice dimension of the sacraments. As James White notes, "the sacraments are intimately connected with justice since sacraments provide means of acting out relationships by enfleshing them in visible forms."[14] Moreover, he argues, the foundation of this "acting out" of justice relationships lies in the rite of baptism, "the sacrament of equality."[15] This fundamental baptismal equality, he continues, then challenges the whole sacramental practice of the church. By contrast, Sri Lankan priest Tissa Balasuriya takes the eucharist as a paradigm for just relations, especially as a model for mutual sharing and social liberation: "The Eucharist was meant to be a symbol, a commemoration and a participation in Jesus' liberative action."[16] He also notes the distortion of the sacrament into a rite that confirms rather than challenges the evils of clericalism, consumerism, racism, sexism, and colonialism, and challenges the church to renew its eucharistic practice to express the love and justice of Christ. White finds the eschatological dimension of the eucharist, as a foretaste of the age of messianic peace and justice, the aspect most clearly related to justice. For David Power, the sacraments themselves are "transformational" when celebrated with full metaphorical use of language, in ways that are adequate to human experience, and in solidarity with those who suffer.[17] However, whatever is identified as the basic paradigm, there is evidently within the liturgical movement a desire to find in the Christian sacraments living witness for active involvement in justice, at the same time that there is an increased awareness that the Christian sacraments have not always borne witness to justice, and have at times justified oppression.

Moreover, there is an intentional critique of the community that is the locus of the sacramental celebrations by some Third-World theologians. Rafael Avila, in *Worship and Politics*, develops this idea of the socio-political context of the celebration of the eucharist in Latin America and concludes that "at this historical moment the only legitimate context for the eucharist—a eucharist such as we have proposed—is one in solidarity with the movement for the liberation of our continent." Such a eucharist, he argues, is both a commemoration and a prophetic sign of liberation, not an abstract or spiritualized idea of liberation, either, but the ongoing struggle to create "objective conditions that will make fellowship, justice, and peace possible."[18] Thus liturgical renewal depends upon and to some degree follows upon a change in the community's priorities, that is, an open determination to commit the community to the struggle for liberation.

THE FEMINIST LITURGICAL MOVEMENT AND THE SACRAMENTS

Feminist activists have long recognized and claimed the equality that seems to be given in baptism, linking baptismal equality and dignity especially with women's struggle for ordination. As was noted above, the biblical text that provides authority for this view of baptism is Galatians 3:27-28, in which Paul quotes a baptismal formula that explicitly links Christian baptism with the rejection of all sorts of social inequality, including sexual inequality.[19] Moreover, the action of the rite itself, which makes no distinction between women and men, strongly witnesses to equality as a baptismal gift. How does it happen, then, that the promises offered in baptism are not realized? If baptism is the constitutive rite of the church, the event whereby Christians are made and the church regenerated, how does the church come to be a patriarchal institution? As Elisabeth Schüssler Fiorenza makes clear in her feminist study of Christian origins, ambivalence on the part of church leaders about radical baptismal equality is found already in the writings of Paul:

> Paul's impact on women's leadership in the Christian mission-ary movement is double-edged. On the one hand he affirms Christian equality and freedom. . . . On the other hand, he subordinates women's behavior in marriage and in the worship assembly to the interests of Christian mission, and restricts their rights not only as "pneumatics" but also as "women," for we do not find such explicit restrictions on men *qua* men in the worship assembly.[20]

Thus the rite of baptism does not accomplish the equality it is witness to, but it is prophetic and empowering. It calls the community forward continually in the struggle to realize its own baptismal character as a community of equals "in Christ."

However, one does not find this eschatological and prophetic emphasis in much contemporary writing on a renewed understanding of baptism. Those concerned with renewing the profound and life-transforming character of baptism in the face of a prevailing devaluation of and disinterest in the rite often emphasize the primacy of God's (or Christ's) action in baptism. Such a strategy has much to recommend it, especially to anyone who has ever witnessed the enervating effect on Christian community and mission brought about by a casual or careless appropriation of baptism. Lack of attention to the radical seriousness of baptism is no doubt a major factor in the church's record of failing to live up to the baptismal promises of equality. However, the emphasis on the primacy of God's work in baptism may obscure the prophetic and priestly demands laid on us by our baptisms, rendering the Christian passive rather than empowering her for action. Representing the extreme view on this emphasis is James White, who finds in baptism the root of Christian equality, but equality of a strangely passive kind. "In short, all those initiated into the body of Christ through baptism are equals because all are passive recipients of God's self giving. At whatever age we come, we are still dependent children, receiving what God freely offers."[21] Such a view of baptism leaves no room for the radical social equality expressed in the Galatians baptismal formula and intuited by Christian feminists, nor does it grant as baptismal *birthright* the necessity of engaging in continual struggle to bring the church and the world into harmony with the baptismal vision of equality.

A more nuanced view is found in the writing of Aidan Kavanagh, who is able to speak of the transformative character of the baptismal event:

> In this cleansing passage through the rites of baptism in its fullness ordinary conventions, social patterns, and ways of perception are suspended, altered, reversed, and transcended. . . . Baptism in its fullness is the primary liminal experience during which the Church is shaped each paschal season into a *communitas* of equals in one Body of neither Jew nor Greek, master nor slave, male nor female, and is prepared to receive fresh and new God's grace in Jesus the Anointed One now become life-giving Spirit.[22]

According to this understanding of baptism it is a turning point in a serious process of conversion (Kavanagh calls the catechumenate "conversion therapy") whereby both baptisand and congregation are engaged in the process of conversion. It depends on a rigorous practice of adult baptism. Thus the catechumen is not rendered the passive, infantile subject of God's work, but rather becomes a member of a group "that discharges a true ministry in the Church by witnessing constantly to the Church her need for continuing conversion in Christ."[23]

Ruether, in her discussion of the ecclesiology of women-church, also wishes to emphasize conversion in the context of a discussion of baptism:

> Conversion is breaking free of the alienating and oppressive socialization that has distorted our consciousness into accepting the normalcy of victimization. Conversion is a leap to a new consciousness that renounces the ideologies that sought to justify these systems of oppression and seeks an alternative world where truthful and good relationships prevail. . . . This means that, as the Anabaptist tradition asserted, the decisive rite of baptism should take place as a proclamation of adult conversion. It is only then that the full reality of baptism is existentially present.[24]

Although she does not speak of catechumenate or "conversion therapy," she does suggest a "period of reflection of several weeks" before baptism, during which time the expertise of those with skills in social and theological analysis could be offered for guidance.[25] Underlying Ruether's position on baptism in women-church, however, is a sectarian and, to some extent, separatist, view of women-church. The church, she says, is "the community of liberation from patriarchy," a "feminist counterculture," an "exodus community." Although she asserts that this understanding of women-church as a separate community is temporary and pragmatic, and should not be confused with ideological separatism,[26] the sectarian tendencies of such a view become evident in her reliance on an Anabaptist view of baptism and her choice of terms such as "exodus" and "counterculture." While no one would deny the significance of the radical witness that sectarian groups such as the Anabaptists, the Shakers, and the Quakers have exercised on our culture and on Christianity, women especially must be cautious about the marginalization that sectarianism imposes. Images of counterculture or renunciation imply a voluntary movement to the margins. However, women are already involuntarily marginalized in the church (even within some sectarian groups) and in the culture. Therefore we do not need to move out any farther; if we are to *exodus* it must be an exodus out of marginality and into the center: the term *eisodus* would seem to be a better expression of our claiming the center. A similar difficulty affects Kavanagh's appropriation of Victor Turner's theory of religious conversion as "liminal." As Caroline Walker Bynum has noted, Turner's theory seems to rely on a form of Christianity that has characterized elites—"educated elites, aristocratic elites, and male elites":

> Thus liminality itself—as fully elaborated by Turner—may be less a universal moment of meaning needed by human beings as they move through social dramas than an escape for those who bear the burdens and reap the benefits of a high place in the social structure. . . . It is the powerful who express imitation of Christ as (voluntary) poverty, (voluntary) nudity, and (voluntary) weakness. But the involuntary poor usually express their *imitatio Christi* not as wealth and exploitation but as struggle.[27]

Similarly, the involuntarily marginal—women—must express our baptismal right and responsibility as struggle for the transformation of the church, the world, and ourselves. Baptism must be the moment not of our moving *out* of, but of our moving *into*, the center of the church, witnessing constantly to the church's need for conversion. Indeed, by moving into the center, women begin to bring into being the paschal community that is truly a community of equals. The church can be said to be a liberated community only in an eschatological sense; that is, only insofar as it is continually struggling to overcome its patriarchy and androcentrism, only insofar as it openly confesses and repents of its sexism, racism, and classism, only insofar as it challenges patriarchal structures in the world.

This is not to say that women-church as worshiping communities of women must not exist. On the contrary, such communities are essential not only to provide communities of solidarity and challenge for women, but also to preserve the church in its wholeness. "The church of women does not share in the fullness of church," Schüssler Fiorenza acknowledges, "but neither do exclusive male hierarchical assemblies."[28] As long as the church remains patriarchal, women-church is necessary as it offers the only context in which women can truly exercise their baptismal office as church: "Just as we speak of the church of the poor, of an African or Asian church, of Presbyterian, Episcopalian, or Roman Catholic churches, without relinquishing our theological vision of the universal Church, so we may speak of the church of women as a manifestation of this universal Church."[29] Our baptism, then, is baptism into this universal church, lived out in women-church, charged to bring about transformation; not baptism out of patriarchy.

Feminist critique of eucharistic practice parallels that of baptism. Eucharist claims to be a sacrament of unity and communion, an enacted sign of the presence of Christ in the midst of the gathered community. However, by restricting women's access to the altar as presiders, as assistants, and even as communicants, because of our femaleness, the sacrament of unity is made into a sacrament of division and alienation, and the authority of Jesus is invoked in order to protect male clerical privilege. Although recent debate in some churches about the legitimacy of women's ordination has in many ways focused unhelpful attention and energy on clerical power, in other ways it has been very revealing. Surveys of ancient as well as contemporary arguments against women's priestly ordination (which has meant in practice the right and authority to preside at the eucharistic table) demonstrate the depth of the church's patriarchy as no other debate in the church has. The arguments are varied: women are unfit for ordination because of the order of creation (Genesis 2); because of women's part in the Fall (Genesis 3); because women are "naturally" under subjection to men; because women do not resemble Christ; because women are ritually unclean due to menstruation and/or childbirth; because women are too sexual and ordination would present an occasion for sin; because women are physically, morally, intellectually, and emotionally weak; because women's proper role is motherhood, not priesthood; because it is women's nature to be passive, not active, receptive, not initiatory; because Jesus did not ordain any women; and so on.[30]

149

By the diverse and in some cases contradictory nature of the arguments, it is clear that no historical or theological reasons can be advanced aside from the acknowledgment that the church, as a patriarchal institution, cannot tolerate women acting at the center of the church's life. As Schüussler Fiorenza observes, "The Eucharist has become the ritual symbolization of the structural evil of sexism."[31] Such recognition has led to a serious dilemma for feminist Christians: "How then can women or anyone for that matter consciously participate in the perpetuation and celebration of structural sin? But how can we be Church without celebrating the Eucharist?"[32] This dilemma has led Catholic feminists to celebrate their own eucharistic meals independently of male authority as a sign that women too are church. For Protestant women whose communities have grudgingly admitted them to ordained ministry, eucharistic presidency carries less symbolic weight. In general, the less importance a tradition places on the observance of the Lord's Supper, the less concern there is about women's presidency at the table.[33] However, insofar as the community that celebrates the eucharist still perpetuates in some degree the "structural evil of sexism," the dilemma exists and must be answered. Since all Christian communities in different degrees perpetuate sexism and racism, all must examine not only their eucharistic practice narrowly defined (that is, who presides, who receives, and under what conditions, as well as questions of language and imagery) but also the extent to which the community that gathers around the table is engaged in struggling against the evils of racism and sexism.

We have seen the extent to which this emphasis on the nature of the community that celebrates has influenced the thought of Third-World liberation theologians. But such emphasis is to be found also among western theologians as well as in the shape of the liturgy itself. The eucharist, among other things, is an expression of and a creator of *koinonia*, that experience of trust and community which forms the basis for a shared meal in any culture.[34] The assumption that this basic trust and community are necessary prerequisites to gathering around the eucharistic table is vividly expressed in the liturgical action of the kiss of peace, which takes for its authority Matthew 5:23-24: "So if you are offering your gift at the altar, and there remember that your brother [or sister] has something against you, leave your gift there before the altar and go; first be reconciled to your brother [or sister], and then come and offer your gift." This most ancient and radical liturgical element attests to the same concern for justice among the members of the Christian community that is found in Paul's letter to the church at Corinth, in which he charges them with "eating and drinking judgement on themselves" for their failure to treat one another justly.[35] Therefore the eucharistic practice of the churches today stands under the same sort of judgment since it fails to "discern the body" in the bodies of women and in the Body of women-church.[36]

Therefore the view that the eucharist is emancipatory because it offers a "foretaste of that just Kingdom where all will be accorded their due"[37] must be measured by the extent to which the community that gathers for this feast is actively engaged in doing justice for women, which means struggling against "powers and principalities." Unless the eschatological banquet of justice and plenty is something we are struggling to bring about and not just longing for, this dimension of the eucharist is tamed, and reduced into "pie-in-the-sky" piety that supports the status quo. In order for the radical social and political implications of the eschatological dimension of the eucharist to be realized, they must be actualized both within the ritual celebration and in the larger context in which the church exists.

FEMINIST SACRAMENTAL QUESTIONS

In an essay entitled "Taking Women Students Seriously," Adrienne Rich poses a question:

"Suppose we were to ask ourselves, simply: What does a woman need to know?" Does she not, as a self-conscious, self-defining human being, need a knowledge of her own history, her much-

151

politicized biology, an awareness of the creative work of women of the past, the skills and crafts and techniques and powers exercised by women in different times and cultures, a knowledge of women's rebellions and organized movements against our oppression and how they have been routed or diminished?[38]

Rich is speaking in the context of university education of women, and the question is made all the more poignant by the knowledge that it is rarely, if ever, asked in such contexts. It also provokes us to ask it of the church as well, especially of the kind of experiential knowledge transmitted by the Christian sacraments. Suppose we were to ask, simply: what do women in the church need to know? The four things that Rich identifies as necessary to women's learning we have already considered from a theological perspective in foregoing chapters. Women need not only a knowledge of our history, but also a theological and liturgical appropriation of our memory, a woman's *anamnesis* at the heart of our liturgical remembering. Women need not only the knowledge of our biology, but an understanding of our bodies and their functions as manifestations of God. Women need to know of women's creative work in order to begin the work of reconstructing our imaginations to include the vision of women as powerful and free. We need not only to know of women's struggles against oppression of past and present, but also to experience a sense of solidarity with those struggles as empowering our own.

These questions are sacramental questions because they have to do with questions of identity and survival, which are finally what baptism and eucharist are about. They are sacramental because they ask what women's experiences of struggle with identity and survival have to do with God, or more precisely, what God has to do with women's struggles. There is more: because the Christian sacraments proclaim, remember, and present Christ, they ask what does Christ have to do with women's struggles for self-determination and survival. If the Christian sacraments are silent on these questions, then Christianity can only be destructive for women, then Christ is not present for women, then God does not remember us. What women need to know from the sacraments of baptism and eucharist is that Christ is present in our struggle to live out our baptismal equality and dignity, and that God has not forgotten us.

Feminist emancipatory sacraments, if they are to be true revelations, true *mysteria*, must reveal God's self-disclosure in women's lives. The loci for this feminist revelation are found in women's struggle for survival and dignity; in the rich and complex particularity of women's lives, influenced both for joy and for sorrow by gender, race, class, nationality; in women's experiences of embodiment; in the sense of connectedness with all that is, especially the common, the everyday, the overlooked; and in women's experiences of love of self and of other women. From these experiences, we know that God has not forgotten us, and we learn to "love her fiercely."

FEMINIST EMANCIPATORY BAPTISM

Baptism is an initiatory rite, but we must take care not to confuse the process of intiation with the momentary event of water baptism. As both historical reconstruction and contemporary reclamation make clear, the event of water baptism stands at the center of a sometimes lengthy and preferably rich and complex process of preparation, education, decision making, "conversion-therapy," ritual participation, and spiritual formation. The process ideally begins long before the rite of water baptism and continues for a lifetime, it is hoped. This recovery of the experience of "baptism in its fullness" offers rich possibilities for a feminist reclamation of baptism. Such a reclamation can and must go beyond earlier practices, however, whether those of the Reformation or those of the ancient church, since there is no period in the church's history when it has been free from sexism.

A feminist emancipatory understanding of baptism must emphasize neither passivity nor exile but empowerment. For women this means the power to claim equality and freedom for ourselves and to work in solidarity with all women in our struggles.

For men, this means the power to challenge the abuse of power by men and to stand in solidarity with women and all who struggle against oppression. For both, to the extent they benefit from structures of racism and classism, it means the power to challenge and to work to change structures and institutions that perpetuate oppression of any kind. This empowerment for change is not limited to the "world" but must also include the church, since it is not a "pure" community but an institution that also perpetuates sexism, racism, and classism.

Since empowerment is best understood as a lifelong process, the ancient catechetical model has much to offer, if it is claimed for feminist reconstruction. According to this model, the process moves though several successive stages of mostly flexible length.[39] The first stage is that of inquiry, when the gospel of equality and freedom is proclaimed and witnessed to by those engaged in the ongoing struggle to live it out. This is the church engaged in mission. The next stage is the catechumenate itself, wherein the inquirer states her intention to join her struggle with the church's struggle for freedom and equality. During this period (of length to be determined by context and circumstances) the catechumens, or *learners*, are welcomed as Christians and engage in a process not only of learning but also of formation and transformation. Admission to this stage expects that the catechumens will have already demonstrated "visible change in their life,"[40] which might take the form of engagement in personal or social change. Admission to the catechumenate may be ritualized by liturgies of examination and welcome. The reception of catechumens into the church can be enacted by calling them by name (at the entrance to the church's worship space, perhaps), asking them to state their intentions, signing them on the forehead and perhaps elsewhere, and welcoming them into the community. These rituals are best done by the community into which the catechumens ask admission, its leaders, and those who will go through the process of initiation most closely with them (traditionally, the sponsors or godparents).

The catechumenate itself should be a time of training and preparation for the struggle, and therefore must include some information about the history of women's struggles in the church and in society. Here the more educational dimensions of Adrienne Rich's questions may be addressed, by instructing candidates for baptism in the history of women in Judaism and Christianity, in the sacredness of women's bodies, in the tradition of women's creative work and leadership, and in the stories of women's struggles against oppression within the church. Since, as Rich observes, our lack of knowledge of these things "has been the key to our powerlessness," then an essential part of a process of empowerment requires such remedial education.[41]

Current writings on the renewed catechumenate, however, constantly stress that education in the narrow sense does not exhaust the purpose of the catechumenate. Kavanagh's term "conversion therapy," although perhaps too individualistic, suggests the deeper purposes of this period of Christian life. Experiential activities, in addition to the education proposed above, should be included in empowerment training. These might include participation in services such as rape crisis centers, women's clinics, women's shelters, or day care centers. Or it might include organizing for political change to benefit women. It might mean similar kinds of women-centered work in church-related settings, especially where the beneficiaries are the poorest and most oppressed women. Together with such solidarity-oriented work, the catechumenate must also lead catechumens into feminist spiritual disciplines designed to construct feminist imagination and to motivate feminist ways of living in the world.

During this period the catechumens may be strengthened in their training and growth by participation in celebrations of scriptural liturgies ("Services of the Word"), blessings and exorcisms, and "rites of transition," which may include anointings or rites of presentation of foundational expressions of the faith (traditionally, the Creed and the Lord's Prayer). In a catechumenate oriented toward the empowerment of women, services of the word might take the form of liturgies shaped by feminist typological appropriation of scripture stories of women such as those considered in chapter 5. Blessings and exorcisms are rites that are particularly associated with empowerment, and thus would be especially fitting during the catechumenate. Such blessings, however, would of necessity be feminist blessings as described by Janet Walton: "[T]he action must be participatory both in word and gesture. Its content must emphasize women's strength, courage, and faithfulness. Its meaning must convey an image of woman whose love embraces and extends a vision of freedom"[42] Such blessings are not something given by one person to another, but shared among the community. Therefore reciprocal rather than dominant gestures are required. Exorcisms offer an opportunity to name the evils of sexism, racism, and classism, and to enable the catechumens to begin to identify the manifestations of these evils in their own lives, as well as empowering them to struggle against them. Anointings are also empowering gestures that have a rich complex of meaning including exorcism, healing, strengthening, and giving of divine power.[43] Especially anointing of the body or of the senses can be a powerful sign of the value of women's bodies in contrast to our culture's devaluation and exploitation of women's bodies, and to the church's historic fear of women's bodies.

Although this process of catechesis may take as long as necessary, the final stage of the process is associated with the period of the church year called Lent, during which time the disciplines undertaken by the catechumens as they prepare for the waters of baptism are adopted by the community of the faithful, acting in solidarity with the catechumens as well as reminding themselves of the ongoing nature of their own baptismal vows. During Lent, then, the entire congregation may take on emancipatory disciplines as a regular means of renewing their determination to live out their baptismal equality on a day-to-day basis.

As the climax to the Lenten-catechumenal preparation is the Paschal celebration itself, the Three Holy Days *(Triduum Sacrum)* wherein the church recalls the death of Jesus as a political criminal and religious heretic, his burial, and his resurrection into new life and freedom. Within this context of recollection, the catechumens make their final binding vows, rejecting evil and claiming the freedom of Jesus, pass through the waters of death, birth, and liberation, and receive the priestly and messianic anointing that empowers them to go forth "in the angry power of the Spirit, . . . sent forth to feed, heal, and liberate our own people who are women."[44] Because this activity is an ongoing struggle, the practice of post-baptismal *mystagogy*, or instruction in the sacramental mysteries and their feminist emancipatory significance, normally follows the central event of baptism, taking place during the Fifty Days of Easter. This is an important sign not only of the lifelong nature of the struggle that begins with entry into the catechumenate but also of the church's intention to support rather than hinder newly baptized persons' intentions to live as free and equal women and men in the world, and in the church itself. Thereby the church signals its intention to be a church *semper reformanda*.

The baptismal rite itself, as well as its larger liturgical context, must reflect the use of emancipatory language and images and emancipatory biblical typology. Feminist imagination and feminist memory must be intentionally engaged, since baptism is the rite of initiation and therefore expresses and embodies the church's identity, even while it is creating the church. In particular, this means: (1) claiming the value of women's bodies by the full and respectful use of the signs of washing, anointing, and clothing; (2) evoking women's bonds and heritage by remembering the names of women in prayers and making explicit connections with women's struggles and the church's solidarity with them; (3) emphasizing baptism as empowerment by naming sexism, racism, classism, and other forms of oppression as evil to be struggled against and by claiming the transformative, eschatological character of baptism.

To some extent, these emphases are found implicitly in the central New Testament motifs of baptism.[45] Baptism as empowerment is suggested by the motif of union with Jesus Christ and with Christ's work (Galatians 3:27-28; Romans 6:3, 5), the gift of the Holy Spirit (Acts 2:1-21; John 3:5; Titus 3:5), and reception into a messianic, prophetic priesthood (I Peter 2:4-5, 9-10). Liturgically, this emphasis has been associated with anointing and laying on of hands, for which we have, as noted in chapter 2, a New Testament warrant in the story of the woman who anoints Jesus before his death. Use of this story typologically in baptism also provides a connection with women's bonds and heritage and relates Jesus' command to "remember" this woman to the church's fundamental identity. Baptism as solidarity with women and all oppressed people is also implied in the ecclesiastical motif of baptism as incorporation into Christ's body on earth (I Corinthians 12:13). When this body is understood not as the hierarchy or institutional structures of the church but as the church of women and the church of the oppressed and the church of those who struggle for survival and dignity, then "incorporation into Christ's body" takes on the same identification with the outcast as did Jesus' life. A related emphasis on baptism as transformational is implied in the motifs of new birth (John 3:5) and forgiveness of sins and reconciliation (I Corinthians 6:11; II Corinthians 5:17-18). Both motifs express the hope of transformation and the possibility for a new order of things to which baptism bears witness. For the church of women this must include the hope for an order in which women and the children dependent on them are safe, fed, clothed, and housed; in which women are free to find "the work our souls must have,"[46] and free to do it; in which women's lives, heritage, and bonds with one another are reverenced; in which women's moral and spiritual agencies are recognized.

Much is made by some contemporary liturgical commentators of the fact that the historical baptismal rites contain many explicit and implicit references to conception, gestation, and childbirth. "New birth is the most explicitly feminine of the biblical images [for baptisms]," observes James White. "The font may be the most female sign the church has."[47] Granted that these images are female, to what extent are they feminist? Baptism certainly has referents in experiences that in traditional societies belong almost exclusively to women: birth, bath, clothing, death, and burial. The extent to which the baptismal font is interpreted as a womb in the traditional baptismal liturgies is impressive.[48] The catechetical period of preparation for baptism is often described by ancient writers as gestation, to be completed by birth through the uterine waters of the baptismal font.[49] Central to this understanding, of course, is the image of church as mother.

Although this would seem to be a potentially powerful female image, several problems with it as a central image for feminist emancipatory sacraments may be observed. First, although the church is imaged as mother, and the baptismal rites imaged as childbirth, the church is led by an all-male hierarchy, its theology and practice shaped, moreover, by men who are for the most part celibate and childless. Thus the image of mother here reflects the images of male clergy rather than women who are or might be mothers. By the same tradition these female acts are performed in the church by men only or at least primarily (women were not allowed to baptize even under emergency situations until the eleventh century).[50] Even though the activities ascribed to God in baptism, especially giving birth, are female, the visible actor, the minister, is normally a man, and the language used to refer to this God who gives birth is male. Further, and even more significant, in spite of this female imagery associated with baptism, the church traditionally came to regard human sexuality and especially female sexuality as dangerous and childbirth as defiling. Indeed, one might well argue that in appropriating childbirth imagery for baptism, the patriarchal church implicitly devalues actual women's lived experience of pregnancy and childbirth, suggesting that the nature event must be supplemented, if not supplanted, by birth into mother church. Moreover, since motherhood is the only explicitly female image found in the church's liturgical tradition, it runs the risk of becoming an umbrella image for women's lives, in spite of the fact that not all women are or choose to be mothers, and that even those who are mothers are also other things as well. Thus it becomes clear that in a patriarchal institution the image of motherhood fails to be emancipatory for women, serving instead subtly to devalue the real-life experience of women who are mothers and to reinforce a patriarchal definition of motherhood. The emancipatory potential of the image of motherhood associated with baptism can be realized only when it is made one of several explicitly female images embodied in liturgy, when women are engaged in giving as

159

well as receiving baptism, and when women's lived experiences
of childbirth are allowed to inform the image.

FEMINIST EMANCIPATORY EUCHARIST

Most contemporary reforms of sacramental practice and faith
emphasize the eucharist as the culmination of the rites of initiation
and as a regular (preferably weekly) renewal of baptism.
Therefore the themes of empowerment, valuation of women's
bodies and lives, transformation and hope for women, and
solidarity with the struggles of the most oppressed women of the
world are also the themes of the eucharistic feast. Where baptism is
imaged as birth, the eucharist becomes the primary and ongoing
nourishment that sustains life. Where baptism is imaged as
crossing of the Red Sea, a passing from slavery into freedom, the
eucharist becomes the meal of freedom, the messianic banquet. As
with the birthing image of baptism, the nursing and meal images
also rely on women's traditional activity, but defined within a
patriarchal context and enacted by men. And also as with baptism,
these images can be emancipatory for women only as they are
depatriarchalized, by becoming part of a larger context of images
reflecting women's work in the world, by women's participation in
giving as well as receiving the meal, and by allowing women's lived
experiences to inform the images of nursing and feeding.

The traditional theological emphases of the eucharist offer
places where feminist memory and imagination can expand
the meaning of eucharist so that its emancipatory potential can
be realized more fully. Seven New Testament motifs of
eucharist may be identified: joyful thanksgiving, *anamnesis,
koinonia,* sacrifice, the presence of Christ, the action of the
Holy Spirit, and the eschatological banquet.[51]

In joyful thanksgiving *(eucharistia)* the church blesses not bread
and wine but Goddess herself for her mighty acts. Because the
shape of the eucharistic prayer is oriented toward thanksgiving to
God (the form of which is derived from Jewish prayer-forms), and
because God's power to act (in the past and therefore in the
present) is central to the prayer, it is important for the prayer to

give thanks to the Deity imaged and addressed as female. This expresses the empowerment given in Baptism by confirming women's power to act in the image of God. In thanking Goddess for her mighty acts in the past, we remember what she has done. This *anamnesis* must include the memory of God's dealing with women in the past as basis for the claim that God continues to deal with women in the present. In remembering women before Goddess, the church fulfills Jesus' command to act "in memory of her," in memory not only of the women who recognized Jesus' messianic mission, but also in memory of all the women who have acted in God's name. The recalling and making present of the memory of women generates *koinonia*, the community that transcends time and space to include all of the "company of heaven." Celebrated within this community are the bonds of women with one another and their solidarity with the struggles of all women. The experience of and commitment to solidarity with the poorest and most despised women of the world recalls the sacrifice of Christ and demands sacrifice from the gathered community.

Sacrifice is a profound expression of solidarity when undertaken voluntarily and on behalf of someone else. It fails to carry the same message when forced on those who are already expected to have nothing. As with the image of servant for those who are regarded as natural servants, the idea of sacrifice carries no transformative message for those, like women, who are expected to be sacrificial by nature. However, two things may be said of the sacrifice demanded by an emancipatory eucharist. First, the sacrifice is, as the eucharist is, a communal rather than an individual act. The whole community of the church is called upon to sacrifice on behalf of the poorest women of the world. Second, sacrifice must aid the struggle of women for survival and dignity. Those who benefit from the oppression of women are called upon to sacrifice their privilege where it will benefit women. Since some women are also in some ways beneficiaries of not only sexism but also racism and classism, we too are called upon to sacrifice our privilege where it will benefit the struggle of women in general. The ability to offer such sacrifice demands a high degree of discernment and the knowledge of intersecting oppressions. It also demands an understanding of the ways in which a patriarchal ideology of sacrifice has sustained sexism and racism. This is particularly critical for women, who have often been called upon to sacrifice ourselves, or have been sacrificed against our wills. As Barbara Andolsen observes:

> For privileged white women, renunciation of unjust race and class privilege is a part of the hard task confronting us. However, even a strategy of renunciation requires careful moral discernment. In what concrete instances should power which we wield as a result of racial and/or class privilege be renounced and in which instances should such power be retained and directed in the service of just goals?[52]

Therefore an emancipatory use of the eucharistic motif of sacrifice must be informed by critical consciousness about both the demand for sacrifice of unjust power and the complexity of interlocking oppressions.

Christ's presence in the gifts of bread and wine has been the focus of great theological controversy for centuries, but contemporary eucharistic theology also emphasizes Christ's presence in the gathered community. In this sense, then, the church of women becomes the evidence of Christ's body in the world, as the bread and wine are the products of the labor of women and men. The image of the body of Christ as present in bread and wine also evokes the bodies and blood of women, whose labor sustains life. It also evokes, as a truthful image of women's lives, the reality of women's bodies broken and blood shed in acts of violence, directed at them because they are women. It also evokes the cultural and traditionally religious fear and hatred of women's bodies and women's blood. As a recollection both of the suffering and death of Christ and of the suffering and death of countless women, the presence of the body in the bread and wine becomes an occasion for lament. As evidenced in the gathered community, the presence of Christ becomes an occasion for thanksgiving and hope, since it is the gathered community that, in the power of the

Spirit, goes forth to "feed, heal, and liberate women." As in baptism, so in the eucharistic meal the action of the Holy Spirit not only transforms bread and wine into body and blood, but she also transforms suffering and brokenness into solidarity and hope. Thus the *epiclesis* is not only or even primarily a request for a change in the bread and wine, but a request for a change in us, the gathered community, that we may be empowered to live out our baptismal freedom. It is this Spirit-led change that makes it possible for us to imagine a world in which all women are free and powerful, in which all women have plenty. "The decision to feed the world / is the real decision," writes Adrienne Rich: "No revolution / has chosen it. For that choice requires / that women shall be free."[53] The eucharist as echatological feast offers imaginative hope, the visionary experience of the goal toward which we work in our daily struggle.

In order for this imaginative and transformative work to affect our sacramental practice and faith, the experiences of women's lives, in all their complexity, contradiction, and commonness, must be recognized for the numinous events they are, just as our sacramental events must be grounded in the experience of daily working to free all women. Ntozake Shange, in describing her work as a poet, also describes the sacramental work that the church of women must do:

> My work
> attempts to ferret out
> what I know and touch
> in a woman's body . . .
> I discuss the simple reality
> of going home at nite,
> of washing one's body,
> looking out the window
> with a woman's eyes.
> We must learn our common symbols,
> preen them
> and share them with the world.[54]

CHAPTER SEVEN

"THE STRING THROUGH THE MIDDLE"

Feminist Spirituality

During a class discussion on feminist spirituality, a student who was also the mother of an infant daughter brought a child's toy to demonstrate the meaning of spirituality for her. The toy was made out of segmented pieces of colorful plastic loosely strung on a cord. When the end of the cord was pulled, the separate pieces came together to form a smiling clown. Spirituality, for her, was what "pulled it all together."[1]

That, too, is the function of this chapter. It attempts to pull together not only the disparate topics we have considered in the foregoing chapter, not only the two contemporary movements that have motivated our explorations, but also the connections, often ignored, between spirituality and politics, between liturgy and social change. The "string through the middle" is feminist spirituality.

Spirituality, before it is particular disciplines or prayers, is a way of being in the world: a way of living, of knowing, of seeing and hearing. It is wholistic, in the sense that it involves our whole persons: our conscious intellectual life and also our subconscious and non-rational life as well; it involves our physical and sensual existence as well as our mental world. Because our spirituality is our way of being in the world, it is also relational and political. It involves the nature of our relationships with others, with God, with the created world, and with ourselves. It is thus not individualistic, but corporate; not private, but engaged.[2] Our spirituality, then, is always the subtext to any liturgical gathering, and it flows from those gatherings.

To speak of feminist spirituality is to indicate on whose behalf one's spirituality is engaged. It is woman-identified spirituality, a way of being in the world that is ultimately accountable to women. It means keeping Adrienne Rich's question always before us: "With whom do you believe your lot is cast?"[3] It means recognizing that as women our lot is cast with all women. The violent abuse of any woman threatens the freedom of all women. The sexual exploitation of any woman threatens the dignity and value of all women's bodies. The economic exploitation of any woman threatens the independence of all women. The strictures that maintain involuntary motherhood threaten the autonomy of all women. Patriarchal strictures that divide women against women prevent us from recognizing that our lot is cast with each other. As soon as we recognize the reality of the abuses and exploitations of patriarchal society, we realize that we cannot be content with things the way they are, that we must move always toward freedom and wholeness for all women. Therefore feminist spirituality is transformative. It is, briefly, a way of being and living that nourishes love for ourselves and one another as women, is engaged in women's struggle for survival and dignity, and is passionately committed to change.

Feminist spirituality, because it is firmly grounded in the world, recognizes that the world is not a safe place for women. The effects of living in a patriarchal society are dangerous for women and sometimes deadly; they include physical abuse, poverty, denial of intellectual and economic benefits, restriction of employment, and denial of spiritual and psychological autonomy. A feminist spirituality that is accountable to all women must not only empower women to overcome these dangers, but also must empower all people to change the world, to make it a safe place for women. Building a different world, constructing a society in which all women are free, demands a spirituality that is truly emancipatory. It also requires strength of purpose, and a feminist emancipatory spirituality can be a source of such strength.

FEMINIST SPIRITUAL DISCIPLINES

Spiritual disciplines, self-imposed practices intended to strengthen one's life and spirit, have, in traditional religions, been an important way of helping people live their faith in the world. Feminist spiritual disciplines can serve the same purpose, providing structure for feminist emancipatory living in a patriarchal world.

1. *We must identify with other women.* The process of world building is a collective endeavor, and requires the participation of all women. Forming groups of women for support, study, and mutual empowerment not only can be nourishing but also can be a powerful political act. Women together can agree not to be victims, can engage in analysis of the social roots of our common oppression, can challenge the tendency to interpret our oppression in individualistic terms, can challenge ourselves to confront the particularities and complexities of women's lives as affected by race, class, and age. To begin to identify with women, to recognize that our lot is cast with all women, is the first step toward generating a new world.

2. *We must name the world.* Language makes things and experiences visible and helps us to make sense of them. Patriarchal language has rendered women invisible and has interpreted our experiences for us. Language that makes women visible and allows us to interpret our own lives is an essential part of world building. The construction of such language is a difficult task, since it requires honesty and courage. We must be willing to hear the truth of other women's lives, to recognize and speak the truth about our own, and to name patriarchy and oppression as well as courage and dignity where we see them. Silence has not protected us; we must learn to speak.

3. *We must choose our own arena of change and struggle.* For Christian women, the question of staying in the church is a real one, a serious one. Many have chosen to leave and work elsewhere; many others choose to remain. For many of those who do choose to remain, the choice itself is a daily decision, requiring constant reassessment and self-examination. As women, we need to support one another in our choices,

recognizing that transformation is necessary everywhere and that the only free space is that which we create.

4. *We must learn to love ourselves.* Self-love may be a serious sin for men in patriarchal society, but it is rarely a problem for women. We have learned and are rewarded for, at best, conditional and derivative self-love. We need instead the unconditional, liberating self-love that Alice Walker calls "womanist": "Loves music. Loves dance. Loves the moon. *Loves* the Spirit. Loves love and food and roundness. Loves struggle. *Loves* the folk. Loves herself. *Regardless.*"[4] Learning to love ourselves as women is our most difficult and our most necessary task as women living in a patriarchal society. It is the necessary precondition to our survival.

5. *We must recover our collective memory.* We need to know that we are not the first women ever to have struggled to change the world. That we have had to struggle over and over is in part due to the fact that we have been denied the "dangerous memory" of the struggles of our foresisters. Once we have learned to recognize the patterns of struggle, gain, loss, and denial, we are better equipped to transform the world. We are stronger when we can name the ways in which we have defeated our own efforts, as well as the ways in which we have been defeated. We are stronger too when we can remember the ways in which we have succeeded, when we remember what we have won, and at what cost. The recovery of our collective memory reminds us that women have always been engaged in struggle, and that women's struggle to survive with dignity is always a struggle against patriarchy.

In the process of recovering our collective memory as women, we discover the value of learning about and honoring the rich variety and complexity of women's lives in different cultures and races. This discovery can be painful as we confront the ways in which women have contributed to and benefited from the oppression of other women, but only in the recognition and naming of these realities is it possible to build solidarity.

6. *We must learn to imagine a different world.* Our ability to imagine that things could be different and how they could be different is our most powerful tool for change. It can also be

one of our most potent sources of nourishment and encouragement. We can imagine a world in which rape does not exist; a
world in which women are valued and strong and free; a world in
which women's experiences are spoken and heard; a world in
which misogyny is unknown. We can begin to imagine a church in
which women's stories, women's bodies, and women's struggles
are considered part of the sacred tradition of the church. We can
begin to imagine a world in which God is as much like women as
she is like men. Such imagining requires discipline, because our
imaginations have been colonized, and we are timid and fearful
about imagining different possibilities. Such a discipline has been
proposed by Joanmarie Smith, who recommends replacing the
word "God" with "Goddess" in one's prayers and references for
the next thirty days.[5] Only by means of such intentional and
sustained discipline can we begin to stretch our imaginations until
the image of God as female seems familiar, and begin to "shatter
the idolatrous hold on our psyche that the word 'God' has."[6]
Intellectual discussion alone is not sufficient to change our
perception of and relationship with God. Only the sustained use of
female language can begin to yield new appellatives for Goddess.

7. *We must celebrate feminist liturgies and rituals.* This is a
two-sided discipline. On the one hand, women need to be free
to gather together as women-church to lament our losses,
celebrate our joys, remember our history, tell our stories, and
claim our power as women. The experience of solidarity that
comes from participation in groups of women for discussion,
study, or strategy finds its liturgical expression in the worship
of women-church. On the other hand, women also need to be
free to claim the church as our church, to place our griefs and
joys, our stories and memories, at the center of the liturgical
gathering of the whole church. Indeed, this is the only way to
have a whole church, since the church that exists now excludes
women's experience and leadership from its center.

8. *We must be engaged in women's struggle.* However powerful
language and liturgy and ritual are, they must not be confused
with social change. Liturgical change can motivate, empower,
nourish, and legitimate social change, but it is not itself social

change. Changing the language of the liturgy tomorrow will not keep an abusive man from beating his wife. The complex social problems that women face, complicated often by racism, classism, and ageism, demand political and social solutions. Liturgical change that is not accompanied by active engagement on women's behalf in the social and political arena is dangerously deceptive. This does not mean that liturgical change must wait upon social change. In fact, the liturgy must in part embody the imaginative model of that for which we work, and for which we hope. The eschatological dimension of liturgy requires that it be future-oriented, directing our energy to the accomplishment of the realm of Goddess on earth. But unless we are working as well as praying for that accomplishment, we defeat ourselves and frustrate the intentions of God for all humanity.

WHAT CAN MEN DO?

The feminist emancipatory disciplines proposed here are directed toward women. But if we hope to bring about a world and church that are whole, men too must be engaged in the struggle for emancipation. Such a massive task of world building requires the best efforts of all of us.

1. *Men can recognize their own limits.* The work of generating feminist emancipatory liturgy and spirituality is, of necessity, women's work. We must engage in the process of naming, creating, and claiming for ourselves. No one else can do it for us. It is the fact that others have been doing it for us for centuries which is part of the problem we must overcome.

2. *Men can begin to identify with women.* For women, the work of identifying with women is not so much choice as recognition of the fact that our lot is already cast with all women. For men, this identification is a real choice, and one that requires both humility and courage. Patriarchal society does not value men who identify with the oppressed, and such identification will inevitably be costly. Such identifica-

169

tion also requires recognition of the ways in which men have been and continue to be complicit in and to benefit from the oppression of others, and at times may demand the abdication of those benefits.

3. *Men can listen attentively and give space and time.* In a patriarchal society and church, men control space and time. Women need space and time to experiment with telling our own stories, to overcome our tendency to censor our own experience or to tell men what we think they want to hear. Men can give this space and time rather than demanding it for themselves, and can refrain from offering interpretations of what they hear.

4. *Men can use their power on women's behalf.* Men must recognize that they have the greater measure of power and influence in our society and in the church, and that they can use that power and influence to benefit women. They especially can confront other men who use their power against women and they can refuse to participate knowingly in such misuse of power.

"THE SPIDER'S GENIUS"

Traditional models and images for spirituality often speak of spirituality in linear form: as ascent, or ladder, or progressive "stages of growth." Nothing about the feminist liturgical movement, either in this century or in previous ones, however, suggests a smooth pattern of steady growth or ascent. A model that seems to express the struggle of feminist emancipatory spirituality better is that of a spider's web. The spider, spinning her web from her own body, creates a world that feeds and protects her, and is unique and perfectly adapted to her environment.

> Anger and tenderness: the spider's genius
> to spin and weave in the same action
> from her own body, anywhere—
> even from a broken web.[7]

Her web is made, strand by stand, not in a straight line, but woven to fit the space available, a necessary shape. Creation and construction happen together, not sequentially. It is slow work, done a bit at a time, often against great odds in a hostile environment.

> . . . "patiently," they say,
> but I recognize in her
> impatience—my own—
>
> the passion to make and make again
> where such unmaking reigns
>
> the refusal to be a victim
> *we have lived with violence for so long*
>
> Am I to go on saying
> for myself, for her
>
> *This is my body,*
> *take and destroy it?*[8]

The slow and necessary work of feminist emancipatory spirituality and liturgy, done "impatiently," refusing to be victims, is dangerous and subversive to patriarchal structures. Poet Muriel Rukeyser says, "What would happen if one woman told the truth about her life? The world would split open."[9] What would happen if a whole church of women told the truth about their lives? What if the men heard them? Would the church split open? Perhaps then we could begin, men and women together, to spin and weave a new world and a new church.

Each spider web is unique, designed for its particular environment. Feminist spirituality is particular to the women who create it. Race, class, age, religious identity, sexual identity, physical ability, all make up the environment in which feminist spirituality is created. Therefore our spinning and weaving of feminist spirituality must be diverse, and must value its diversity as necessary for our survival. The new world and new church we weave will celebrate diversity over uniformity.

Spider webs, Rich suggests, are produced by a balance of "anger and tenderness": the impatient anger that keeps the spider remaking and reweaving, even from a broken web, and the tenderness with which the spider weaves the fragile strands into a web. Feminist spirituality too requires anger and impatience at the ongoing violence with which women continue to live. It requires tenderness and love for ourselves and other women. The new world and new church we weave will value the power that comes from refusing to be victims and will celebrate women's love of self and one another.

Spider webs are made of interconnected strands. Feminist spirituality weaves together strands of religion and politics, body and mind, action and contemplation, separation and integration, nature and culture. The new world and new church we weave will value interconnectedness and celebrate the whole web of life.

NOTES

INTRODUCTION

1. See Robert Taft, "The Structural Analysis of Liturgical Units: An Essay in Methodology," in *East and West: Problems in Liturgical Understanding* (Washington, D.C.: Pastoral Press, 1984), pp. 152-53, and Aidan Kavanagh, *On Liturgical Theology* (New York: Pueblo Press, 1985), pp. 87-88.

2. See, for example, Letty Russell, *Household of Freedom: Authority in Feminist Theology* (Philadelphia: The Westminster Press, 1987).

CHAPTER ONE

1. Adrienne Rich, *A Wild Patience Has Taken Me This Far* (New York: W. W. Norton, 1981), pp. 3-5.

2. See, for example, in Arlene Swidler, ed., *Sistercelebrations* (Philadelphia: Fortress Press, 1974), "God of the Matriarchs," pp. 1-8; the myth of Lilith in "Sistercelebration: To Cultivate the Garden," pp. 47-55 (and its original full text by Judith Plaskow, "The Coming of Lilith" in Carol Christ and Judith Plaskow, eds., *Womanspirit Rising* [New York: Harper Forum, 1979], pp. 198-209), "The Trial of the Halloween Six" with its naming of women burned as witches, pp. 60-67. More recently, see, in Miriam Therese Winter, *WomanPrayer, WomanSong* (Oak Park, Ill.: Meyer-Stone Books, 1987), "Valiant Women," pp. 115-41; "Out of Exile," pp. 143-61; "Choose Life," pp. 163-72; in Rosemary Radford Ruether, *Women-Church* (New York: Harper & Row, 1985) see "Litany of Remembrance of Foremothers," pp. 142-43; "Hallowmas: Remembrance of the Holocaust of Women," p. 223-26.

3. On the reconstruction of Goddess-worship as a contemporary religion, see especially Carol Christ, "Why Women Need the Goddess" in Christ and Plaskow, *Womanspirit Rising*, pp. 273-87 and Starhawk, *The Spiral Dance: A Rebirth of the Ancient Religion of the Great Goddess* (New York: Harper & Row, 1979). For influence on Christian feminist liturgy, compare "Fire and Flame" in Winter, pp. 49-57 with the Candlemas ritual in Starhawk, pp. 174-75, or see the "Croning ritual" in Reuther, pp. 206-09.

4. Swidler, *Sistercelebrations* p. v.

5. On liturgy being "of God," see especially Aidan Kavanagh, *On Liturgical Theology* (New York: Pueblo Press, 1984), pp. 114-17.

6. Studies on the liturgical movement are numerous. For a useful summary see H. Ellsworth Chandlee, "The Liturgical Movement" in J. G. Davies, ed., *A New Dictionary of Liturgy and Worship* (London: SCM Press, 1986) and the accompanying bibliography.

7. Published collections of feminist liturgies which are inten-

tionally Christian or which include Christian liturgies include Swidler, *Sistercelebrations;* Sharon Neufer Emswiler and Thomas Neufer Emswiler, *Women and Worship* (New York: Harper & Row, 1974); Ruth Duck, ed., *Bread for the Journey* (New York: Pilgrim Press, 1981, 1982); Winter, *WomanPrayer, WomanSong;* Ruether, *Women-Church;* Linda Clark, Marian Ronan, and Eleanor Walker, eds., *Image-Breaking, Image-Building* (New York: Pilgrim Press, 1981).

8. Swidler, *Sistercelebrations,* pp. v-vi.

9. Clark, Ronan, Walker, *Image-Breaking,* p. 8.

10. Swidler, *Sistercelebrations,* p. v.

11. Ibid., p. 81.

12. For example, see the plan for a Women-Church center in Ruether, *Women-Church,* pp. 147-48. The "celebration center" is a "round room" with "no immovable furniture," p. 146.

13. E. M. Broner, "Honor and Ceremony in Women's Ritual," in Charlene Spretnak, ed., *The Politics of Women's Spirituality* (New York: Anchor Press-Doubleday, 1982), p. 234.

14. This confidence is more common in earlier collections as it is in earlier feminist writings. The complexities of women's unity and the difficulty of talking about common experience has recently been eloquently challenged by women of color. See the essays, for example, in Janet Kalven and Mary Buckley, eds., *Women's Spirit Bonding* (New York: Pilgrim Press, 1984).

15. Rosemary Radford Ruether, "The Feminist Liturgical Movement," in Davies, *A New Dictionary,* p. 241.

16. James F. White, *New Forms of Worship* (Nashville: Abingdon Press, 1971), chapters 1-3; *Sacraments as God's Self-Giving* (Nashville: Abingdon Press, 1983), pp. 121-24.

17. *Word and Table: A Basic Pattern of Sunday Worship for United Methodists,* Supplemental Worship Resource 3, 1980 edition (Nashville: Abingdon Press, 1976, 1980), p. 13. See also *The Service for the Lord's Day,* Supplemental Liturgical Resource 1 (Philadelphia: Westminster Press, 1984) and Marion J. Hatchett, *Commentary on the American Prayer Book* (New York: Seabury Press, 1981).

18. *Word and Table,* p. 13.

19. *The Service of the Lord's Day,* p. 150.

20. Ibid., p. 7.

21. Chandlee, "The Liturgical Movement," in Davies, *A New Dictionary.*

22. *The Service of the Lord's Day,* p. 150.

23. *The Constitution on the Sacred Liturgy* (*Sacrosanctum Concilium*), paragraph 14 and *passim.*

24. *The Service of the Lord's Day,* p. 150.

25. On renewal of church space, see, for example, E. A. Sovik, *Architecture for Worship* (Minneapolis: Augsburg, 1973); National Conference of Catholic Bishops, *Environment and Art in Catholic Worship* (Chicago: Liturgy Training Publications, 1986); James F. White and Susan J. White, *Church Architecture: Building and Renovating for Christian Worship* (Nashville: Abingdon Press, 1988).

26. In addition to commentaries on denominational reforms, see Robert Hovda, *Strong, Loving, and Wise: Presiding in Liturgy* (Collegeville: Liturgical Press, 1976); Aidan Kavanagh, *Elements of Rite* (New York: Pueblo Press, 1982).

27. Ruether, *Women-Church,* p. 88.

28. Ibid., pp. 88-89.

29. Kavanagh, *Elements of Rite*, p. 13. See also pp. 12-13, pp. 38-40, pp. 61-62, *passim*.

30. Ruether, *Women-Church*, pp. 89-91.

31. In this light, consider Kavanagh's comment: "That the liturgy is hierarchically structured does not mean that the hierarchy alone do it, but that its doing is the outcome of diverse ministries working in concert for a common end which is never just the liturgical act by itself. The common end for which the diverse liturgical ministries work is not a ceremony but a corporate life in faithful communion with all God's holy people and holy things." *Elements of Rite*, p. 12. Here "hierarchical" is being at least modestly redefined into something more communal than it is normally understood to be. On authority as a particular issue for women, see Letty Russell, *Household of Freedom: Authority in Feminist Theology* (Philadelphia: The Westminster Press, 1987).

32. "There was a time when you were not a slave, remember that. You walked alone, full of laughter, you bathed bare-bellied. You say you have lost all recollection of it, remember . . . you say there are no words to describe it, you say it does not exist. But remember. Make an effort to remember. Or, failing that, invent." Monique Wittig, *Les Guerilleres*, trans. David LeVay (New York: Avon Books, 1971), p. 89. This text is frequently quoted or alluded to in feminist writings. See, for example, Carol Christ, "Why Women Need the Goddess," in Christ and Plaskow, *Womanspirit Rising*, p. 277.

33. Elisabeth Schüssler Fiorenza, *Bread Not Stone: The Challenge of Feminist Biblical Interpretation* (Boston: Beacon Press, 1985), pp. 15-22.

CHAPTER TWO

1. David Power has dealt with the dangers to liturgical celebration in forgetting that which we do not wish to remember, especially in relation to the Holocaust, in "Response: Liturgy, Memory, and the Absence of God," *Worship* 59 (1985), pp. 447–55.

2. "Turning the Wheel 4: Self-Hatred," in *A Wild Patience Has Taken Me This Far* (New York: W. W. Norton, 1981), p. 55.

3. This story provides the paradigm for Elisabeth Schüssler Fiorenza's *In Memory of Her: A Feminist Theological Reconstruction of Christian Origins* (New York: Crossroad, 1983). For an interpretation of the political significance of the event, see pp. xiii-xiv. She does not consider whether the act, as later interpreted by the church, might have had a baptismal significance as well.

4. For example: in the Common Lectionary, the story is part of only the long reading of the Passion on Passion Sunday in Year B and is omitted if the short reading is used. See my article, "Images of Women in the Lectionary," in Elisabeth Schüssler Fiorenza and Mary Collins, eds., *Women Invisible in Theology and Church* (*Concilium* 182, Edinburgh: T & T Clark, 1985), pp. 58-59.

5. M-J LaGrange, "Jésus a-t-il été oint plusieurs fois et par plusiers femmes?", *Revue Biblique* (1912), pp. 504-32; V. Saxer, *Le Culte de Marie-Madeleine en Occident*, 2 vols. (Paris: Cahiers d'Archéologie et d'Histoire, 1959).

6. Schüssler Fiorenza, *In Memory of Her*, p. 153.

7. J. R. Wilkes, "Remembering," *Theology* 84 (March 1981), pp. 87-95.

8. On liturgy and eschatology, see especially Geoffrey Wainwright, *Eucharist and Eschatology* (New York: Oxford University Press, 1981); on eschatology and history,

see Robert Taft, *Beyond East and West: Problems in Liturgical Understanding* (Washington, D.C.: Pastoral Press, 1984), pp. 11-30.

9. See Ralph Keifer, *Blessed and Broken: An Exploration of the Contemporary Experience of God in Eucharistic Celebration* (Wilmington, Del.: Michael Glazier, 1982), pp. 96-108.

10. See Thomas J. Talley, *The Origins of the Liturgical Year* (New York: Pueblo Press, 1985); Tad Guzie, "Liturgical Year: What Does It Mean to Remember?" in *The Church Gives Thanks and Remembers,* Lawrence Johnson, ed. (Collegeville: Liturgical Press, 1984).

11. Taft, *Beyond East and West,* pp. 127-49; cf. pp. 6-11.

12. This is a topic which has produced a vast amount of literature. For a convenient summary of the most significant interpreters, see Fritz Chenderlin, S.J., *"Do This as My Memorial"* (Rome: Biblical Institute Press, 1982). See also Marjorie H. Sykes, "The Eucharist as 'Anamnesis'," *Expository Times* 71 (1960), pp. 115-18; Max. Thurian, *The Eucharistic Memorial,* 2 vols. trans. J. G. Davies (Richmond, Vir.: John Knox Press, 1960, 1961).

13. Brevard S. Childs, *Memory and Tradition in Israel* (London: SCM Press, 1962), p. 33; Chenderlin, pp. 185, 217-22; Sykes, pp. 115, 116.

14. O. Michel, "Mimneskomai," TDNT, pp. 675-76.

15. Sykes, "The Eucharist as 'Anamnesis,' " pp. 116-17.

16. Paul F. Bradshaw, *Daily Prayer in the Early Church* (New York: Oxford University Press, 1982), pp. 35-37.

17. See W. Jardine Grisbrooke, "Intercession at the Eucharist," *Studia Liturgica* IV (1965), pp. 129-55; V (1966), pp. 20-44; pp. 87-103.

18. Dom Bernard Botte, O.S.B., "Problèmes de l'Anamnèse," *Journal of Ecclesiastical History* 5 (1954), pp. 16-24.

19. Ibid., pp. 20-21.

20. Bradshaw, *Daily Prayer,* pp. 12-15.

21. Taft, *Beyond East and West,* pp. 3-4, 7ff.

22. Power, "Worship after the Holocaust," p. 448. It is significant that the "Eucharist in an Age of Abandonment" with which Power concludes this article contains the congregational refrain, "Remember, O God, lest we perish" following the anamnesis, and concludes the intercessions with "Remember, O God, lest we forget," p. 454. See also Carol Christ's powerful article, "Women's Liberation and the Liberation of God: An Essay in Story Theology," in *The Jewish Woman,* Elizabeth Koltun, ed. (New York: Schocken Books, 1976), pp. 11-17.

23. Mary Collins, O.S.B., "Naming God in Public Prayer," *Worship* 59 (1985), p. 301.

24. Ibid., p. 300; see also Gail Ramshaw Schmidt,*"De Divini Nominibus:* The Gender of God," *Worship* 56 (1982), pp. 117-31.

25. Phyllis Bird, "Images of Women in the Old Testament," in Rosemary Radford Ruether, ed., *Religion and Sexism* (New York: Simon and Schuster, 1974), pp. 41-88.

26. Procter-Smith, "Images of Women in the Lectionary," pp. 51-62.

27. Shawn Madigan, in "Called to Be Holy, Made to Be Saints," *Liturgy* 1 no. 2 (1980), notes that the Roman sanctoral is 82 percent male, 81 percent clerical, 78 percent upper class. See pp. 32-36.

28. See Marina Warner, *Alone of All Her Sex* (New York: Random House, 1976); Pamela C. Berger, *The Goddess Obscured* (Boston: Beacon Press, 1985); Rosemary Reuther, *Mary: The Feminine Face of the Church* (Philadelphia: Westminister Press, 1977); Barbara Corrado Pope, "Immaculate and

Powerful: the Marian Revival in the Nineteenth Century," in *Immaculate and Powerful: The Female in Sacred Image and Social Reality*, Clarissa W. Atkinson, Constance H. Buchanan, and Margaret Miles, eds. (Boston: Beacon Press, 1985), pp. 173-200.

29. See Berenice A. Carroll, ed., *Liberating Women's History* (Urbana: University of Illinois Press, 1976); Jo Ann Hackett, "In the Days of Jael: Reclaiming the History of Women in Ancient Israel," in *Immaculate and Powerful*, pp. 15-38; Adela Yarbro Collins, ed. *Feminist Perspectives on Biblical Scholarship* (Chico, Calif.: Scholar's Press, 1985); Letty Russell, ed., *Feminist Interpretation of the Bible* (Philadelphia: Westminister Press, 1985).

30. Phyllis Trible, *God and the Rhetoric of Sexuality* (Philadelphia: Fortress, 1978).

31. Phyllis Trible, *Texts of Terror* (Philadelphia: Fortress, 1984.)

32. *Texts of Terror*, p. 3.

33. Power includes lament in his "Eucharist in an Age of Abandonment," *Worship after the Holocaust*, pp. 450, 452. Trible's *Texts of Terror* concludes the final chapter on Jephthah's daughter in imitation of the annual ritual of the daughters of Israel and mourns her death with a moving poetic lament. See pp. 108-9.

34. (New York: Crossroad Press, 1983), p. 31.

35. Ibid., pp. 33-35.

36. Ibid., p. 343.

37. Ibid., pp. 350-51; cf. "Women-Church: The Hermeneutical Center of Feminist Biblical Interpretation," in *Bread Not Stone: The Challenge of Feminist Biblical Interpretation* (Boston: Beacon Press, 1984).

38. "Women-Church: The Hermeneutical Center of Feminist Biblical Interpretation," pp. 15-22.

39. Cf. *In Memory of Her*, pp. 60-64, especially the "apocryphal letter of Phoebe" reproduced there.

40. Judy Chicago, *The Dinner Party: A Symbol of Our Heritage* (Garden City, N.Y.: Doubleday Anchor Books, 1979); Meinrad Craighead, *The Mother's Songs* (New York: Paulist Press, 1986).

41. See, for example: Marge Piercy, *Living in the Open* (New York: Alfred Knopf, 1976); Judy Grahn, *She Who* (Oakland, Calif.: Diana Press, 1977); Adrienne Rich, *Diving into the Wreck: Poems 1971-72* (New York: W. W. Norton, 1973); *The Dream of a Common Language: Poems 1974-1977* (New York: W. W. Norton, 1978); *A Wild Patience Has Taken Me This Far: Poems 1978-1981* (New York: W. W. Norton, 1981); Ntozake Shange, *For Colored Girls Who Have Considered Suicide When the Rainbow is Enuf* (New York: Macmillan, 1977); Alice Walker, *Horses Make a Landscape Look More Beautiful* (New York: Harcourt Brace Jovanovich, 1984).

42. "Diving into the Wreck," in *Diving into the Wreck*, p. 23; "Natural Resources," p. 64, and "Transcendental Etude," p. 77, in *The Dream of a Common Language*.

43. "Transcendental Etude," p. 74; cf. "The Images," in *A Wild Patience Has Taken Me This Far*, p. 5. In both poems "re-membering" is contrasted with society's "dismembering" of women, literally as well as figuratively.

44. See Ntozake Shange, *For Colored Girls*, pp. 60-63; Alice Walker, *The Color Purple* (New York: Harcourt Brace Jovanovich, 1982), pp. 164-68.

45. Alice Walker, *In Search of Our Mother's Gardens* (New York: Harcourt Brace Jovanovich, 1983), pp. xi-xii.

46. Anne Cameron, *Daughters of Copper Woman* (Vancouver, B.C.: Press Gang Publishers, 1987), preface.

47. Ibid., pp. 62, 150.

48. Ibid., p. 145.

49. Kim Chernin, *The Flame Bearers* (New York: Random House, 1986), p. 270.

50. The question of "lost" vs. "secret" memory is not easily answered. Perhaps "secret" is only another way of saying "lost," and it is in fact all after-the-fact reconstruction. Or perhaps "lost" is a disguise for "secret," and in fact women (and men) have preserved some parts of women's memory, perhaps in part unconsciously. The subversive possibilities of women's traditional gatherings for "gossip," needlework, cooking, etc., have always been recognized. Writers often speak of women's stories and traditions being "hidden" in a patriarchal text. How do we know that the hiding was not purposeful? For a brilliant and witty fictional exposition of this theme, see Suzette Haden Elgin, *Native Tongue* (New York: Daw Books, 1984) and *Native Tongue II: The Judas Rose* (New York: Daw Books, 1987).

51. (New York: Harper & Row, 1985.) Ruether reports only on Christian communities. For information on neopagan women's communities, see Starhawk, *The Spiral Dance* (New York: Harper & Row, 1979) and Margot Adler, *Drawing Down the Moon* (Boston: Beacon Press, 1979; rev. ed., 1986). There are similar activities among Jewish women. See especially Judith Plaskow, "Standing Again at Sinai: Jewish Memory from a Feminist Perspective," in *Tikkun* 1, no. 2, pp. 28-34 and the references cited therein.

52. Ruether, *Women-Church*, pp. 188-89; 200-202; 204-5; 217-21. See also "Prayer on Menstruation" in *Siddur Nashim: A Sabbath Prayer Book for Women*, Naomi Janowitz and Maggie Wenig (Providence: Naomi Janowitz and Maggie Wenig, 1976).

53. Ruether, *Women-Church*, pp. 141-63. See also Carolyn R. Shaffer, "Spiritual Techniques for Re-Powering Survivors of Sexual Assault," in *The Politics of Women's Spirituality*, Charlene Spretnak, ed. (New York: Anchor Press, 1982), pp. 462-69.

54. In his address to the 1983 meeting of the North American Academy of Liturgy, Geoffrey Wainwright called this process "critical archeology," and noted: "More important (if the two matters can be separated) than the attribution of female titles and feminine qualities to God may be the greater integration of Christian women's experience of God into the common rites and texts of the worshiping church." *Worship* 57 (1983), p. 317.

55. See E. Dekkers, "L'Eucharistie, Imitation ou Anamnèse, de la Dernière Cène?" *Revue des Sciences Religieuses* 58, no. 1-3 (1984), pp. 15-23.

56. See Patrick Regan, "The Fifty Days and the Fiftieth Day," *Worship* 55 no. 3, (May 1981) pp. 194-218, and "The Three Days and the Forty Days," *Worship* 54 no. 1 (Jan. 1980), pp. 2-17.

57. For examples of the new appreciation of the role of imagination in theological reflection, see Philip S. Keane, S.S., *Christian Ethics and Imagination* (New York: Paulist Press, 1984); Kathleen R. Rischer, *The Inner Rainbow: The Imagination in Christian Life* (New York: Paulist Press, 1983); Sallie McFague, *Metaphorical Theology* (Philadelphia: Fortress Press, 1982) and *Models of God: Theology for An Ecological, Nuclear Age* (Philadelphia: Fortress Press, 1987); Amos N. Wilder, *Theopoetic: Theology and the Religious Imagination* (Philadelphia: Fortress Press, 1976).

58. G. Bornkamm, "Mysterion," *Theological Dictionary of the New Testament,* pp. 802-28.

59. James F. White, *Sacraments as God's Self-Giving* (Nashville: Abingdon Press, 1983), p. 31.

60. Ibid.

61. Audre Lorde, "Poems Are Not Luxuries," *Chrysalis* 3 (1977), p. 8. For discussion of the significance of imaginative utopian literature for feminism, see *Women in Search of Utopia,* Ruby Rohrlich and Elaine Hoffman Baruch, eds. (New York: Schocken Books, 1984).

62. *In Memory of Her,* pp. xiii-xiv.

63. Ibid., p. xiv.

64. See especially Gabriele Winkler, "The Original Meaning of the Prebaptismal Anointing and its Implications," *Worship* 52 (1978), pp. 24-45.

65. *In Memory of Her,* p. xiv.

CHAPTER THREE

1. For a careful consideration of the problem of human participation in the liturgy, especially in relation to the sacraments, see Regis Duffy, *Real Presence: Worship, Sacraments, and Commitment* (New York: Harper & Row, 1982).

2. Being rendered invisible and voiceless is not the same as *being* invisible and voiceless. In reality, of course, women are neither; we have been hidden and silenced by androcentric and patriarchal culture and institutions.

3. Feminist interpretation of scripture has a stake in both of these demands, since obscuring the often harsh reality of patriarchy does not aid women's struggle to be free of patriarchy. At the same time, where scriptural texts can support women's struggle, they must be allowed to speak clearly, without androcentric restraints. The *Inclusive Language Lectionary* (published for the Cooperative Publication Association by John Knox Press, Atlanta, The Pilgrim Press, New York, and The Westminster Press, Philadelphia) is a commendable example of an attempt to confront in particular the second of these concerns.

4. See the *Inclusive Language Lectionary,* passim.

5. For a thoughtful critique of this formula, see Gail Ramshaw-Schmidt, "Naming the Trinity: Orthodoxy and Inclusivity," *Worship* 60 (1986), pp. 491-98.

6. Ibid.

7. For an interesting example of liturgical inclusive language, see the Eucharistic Prayer for All Saints (Service #13) in *Holy Communion: a Service Book for Use by the Minister* (Nashville: United Methodist Publishing House, 1987), p. 34: "Blessed are you, . . . God of Abraham and Sarah, God of Miriam and Moses, God of Joshua and Deborah, God of Ruth and David . . . God of our mothers and our fathers. . . ."

8. On the process of "degeneration of language," whereby terms are devalued when they shift from referring to men referring to women, see Casey Miller and Kate Swift, *Words and Women* (Garden City, N.Y.: Anchor/Double-day, 1977).

9. Casey Miller and Kate Swift, *The Handbook of Nonsexist Writing for Writers, Editors, and Speakers* (New York: Barnes and Noble, 1980), p. 77.

10. See Rosemary Radford Ruether, *Women-Church: Theology and Practice* (San Francisco: Harper & Row, 1985), passim, especially p. 283, n. 4. For a more thoroughgoing transformation of language, see Mary Daly, *Gyn/Ecology* (Boston: Beacon Press, 1978) and *Pure Lust* (Boston: Beacon Press, 1984).

11. Adrienne Rich, "Transcendental Etude," in *The Dream of a Common Language* (New York: W. W. Norton, 1978), p. 76.

12. Elisabeth Schüssler Fiorenza, *In Memory of Her: A Feminist Theological Reconstruction of Christian Origins* (New York: Crossroad Publishing Company, 1983), p. 349.

13. The literature on the abuse of women in our society is growing rapidly, and only the most important works can be cited here. For a general treatment of the problem see Del Martin, *Battered Wives*, updated edition (New York: Pocket Books, 1983); Susan Brownmiller, *Against Our Will: Men, Women, and Rape* (New York: Simon and Schuster, 1975); Kathleen Barry, *Female Sexual Slavery* (New York: Avon Books, 1981); for a theological-pastoral treatment, see Marie Marshall Fortune, *Sexual Violence: The Unmentionable Sin* (New York: The Pilgrim Press, 1983).

14. See Adrienne Rich, *Of Woman Born: Motherhood as Experience and Institution* (New York: W. W. Norton, 1976).

15. Such liturgies and rituals are widespread. For Christian examples, see Ruether, *Women-Church*, rites of healing from violence, rape, incest, battering, abortion, miscarriage, on pp. 151-63; puberty rite for a young woman, pp. 188-90; birthing preparation ritual, pp. 200-3; menopause liturgy, pp. 204-6.

16. For a discussion of the issues raised by these divisions among women, see *Women's Spirit Bonding*, Janet Kalven and Mary Buckley, eds. (New York: The Pilgrim Press, 1984).

17. Margaret Miles, *Image as Insight: Visual Understanding in Western Christianity and Secular Culture* (Boston: Beacon Press, 1985), pp. 128-29.

18. Ibid., pp. 146-50.

19. Quoted in *Käthe Kollwitz: Jake Zeitlin Bookshop and Gallery, 1937* (Long Beach: California State University, 1979), p. 35. For collections of Kollwitz's work, see August Klipstein, *The Graphic Work of Käthe Kollwitz* (New York: Galerie St. Etienne, 1955); Herbert Bittner, *Käthe Kollwitz Drawings* (New York: Thomas Yoseloff, 1959); Adolf Heilborn, *Käthe Kollwitz* (Berlin: Verlag Konrad Lemmer, 1949); Martha Kearns, *Käthe Kollwitz: Woman and Artist* (Old Westbury, New York: The Feminist Press, 1976).

20. (New York: Paulist Press, 1986.)

21. For further examples of Craighead's work in a more conventionally Christian context, see her illustrations for Miriam Therese Winter, *WomanPrayer, WomanSong* (Oak Park Ill.: Meyer-Stone Books, 1987).

22. Miles, *Image as Insight*, p. 150.

23. (New York: Touchstone, Simon and Schuster, 1977) pp. 2-5, passim.

24. Ibid.; see especially pp. 179-205, and table 5 on p. 181.

25. Ibid., pp. 55-59.

26. Ibid., pp. 196-97.

27. For a discussion of the importance of liturgical language for victims of domestic violence and abuse, see Marjorie Procter-Smith, "'Reorganizing Victimization': The Intersection between Liturgy and Domestic Violence," *Perkins Journal* XL, no. 4 (October 1987), pp. 17-27.

CHAPTER FOUR

1. For a cogent presentation of some of the implications of this observation, see Carol Christ, "Why Women Need the Goddess: Phenomenological, Psychological, and Political reflections," in Carol Christ and Judith Plaskow, eds., *Womanspirit Rising: A Feminist Reader in Religion* (San Francisco and New York: Harper & Row, 1979), pp. 273-87.

2. The difficulties in keeping both of these problems in view is demonstrated by Robert L. Hurd in "Complementarity: A Proposal for Liturgical Language," *Worship* 61 (September 1987), in which he recognizes the problems created by the absence of female referents to God and proposes "the yoking of male and female images of God (for example, 'the womb of the Father')," p. 402. That his proposal fails to take with sufficient seriousness the patriarchal context of male God-language is demonstrated by the example just quoted, which is essentially androcentric, rather than "co-equal." Theories of complementarity fail to take into account the patriarchal context of male God-language and the asymmetry of male and female models.

3. See the work of "symbolic anthropologists" such as Sherry Ortner and Harriet Whitehead, eds., *Sexual Meanings: The Cultural Construction of Gender and Sexuality* (Cambridge: Cambridge University Press, 1981) and Michelle Z. Rosaldo and Louise Lamphere, eds., *Women, Culture, and Society* (Stanford: Standford University Press, 1974). For an important recent study of the relationship between gender and religious symbolism, see Caroline Walker Bynum, Stevan Harrell, and Paula Richman, eds., *Gender and Religion: On the Complexity of Symbols* (Boston: Beacon Press, 1986).

4. Caroline Walker Bynum, "Introduction: The Complexity of Symbols," in *Gender and Religion*, p. 2.

5. Ibid., p. 3.

6. See Mary Collins, "Naming God in Public Prayer," *Worship* 59 (1985), pp. 291-304.

7. Ibid., p. 304.

8. Emily Erwin Culpepper describes the "grass-roots" character of the Goddess-movement: "There is no one prophetess, no single thealogian, no central religious leader, no sacred book, no holy city that establishes or defines what a Goddess orientation is. Of course, this makes the phenomenon difficult to summarize." "Contemporary Goddess Thealogy: A Sympathetic Critique," in *Shaping New Vision: Gender and Values in American Culture*, Clarissa Atkinson, Constance Buchanan, Margaret Miles, eds. (Ann Arbor: UMI Research Press, 1987), p. 52. The same is true, to a large degree, of the Jewish and Christian feminist movements.

9. See Rosemary Radford Ruether, *Sexism and God-Talk: Toward a Feminist Theology* (Boston: Beacon Press, 1983), p. 67; Elizabeth Johnson, "The Incomprehensibility of God and the Image of God Male and Female," *Theological Studies* 45 (1984), p. 443.

10. Adrienne Rich, "The Images," in *A Wild Patience Has Taken Me This Far* (New York: W. W. Norton, 1981), pp. 3-5.

11. In Christ and Plaskow, *Womanspirit Rising: A Feminist Reader in Religion* (San Francisco: Harper & Row, 1979), pp. 273-87.

12. In Christ and Plaskow, *Womanspirit Rising*, p. 172.

13. Joanmarie Smith, "Case for Inclusive Language: A Response," in *Religious Education* 80 (1985), p. 641.

14. See especially Phyllis Trible, *God and the Rhetoric of Sexuality* (Philadelphia: Fortress Press, 1978) and Virginia Ramey Mollenkott, *The Divine Feminine: Biblical Imagery of God as Female* (New York: Crossroad, 1983).

15. On the role of Wisdom in the Hebrew Scriptures, see Claudia V. Camp, *Wisdom and the Feminine in the Book of Proverbs* (Sheffield, England: Almond Press, 1985); on the Christian development of Sophia and Christology, see Elisabeth Schüssler Fiorenza, *In Memory of Her: A Feminist Theological Reconstruction of Christian Origins* (New York: Crossroad, 1983), pp. 130-40. For a contemporary appropriation of this image see Susan Cady, Marian Ronan, and Hal Taussig, *Sophia: The Future of Feminist Spirituality* (San Francisco: Harper & Row, 1986). See also its frequent use in liturgical texts in Ruether, *Women-Church.*

16. Matthew 11:28-30 ("Wisdom's call"); I Corinthians 1:24, 30.

17. See Eleanor McLaughlin, "Women, Power, and the Pursuit of Holiness in Medieval Christianity," in *Women of Spirit: Female Leadership in the Jewish and Christian Traditions,* Rosemary Ruether and Eleanor McLaughlin, eds. (New York: Simon and Schuster, 1979), pp. 99-130; Elaine Pagels, "Whatever Became of God the Mother?" in *Womanspirit Rising,* pp. 107-19; Barbara Brown Zikmund, "The Feminist Thrust of Sectarian Christianity," in *Women of Spirit,* pp. 205-24; Michael A. Williams, "Uses of Gender Imagery in Ancient Gnostic Texts," in *Gender and Religion,* pp. 196-227.

18. For a critique of the Shakers' dualistic theology, see my study, *Women in Shaker Community and Worship: A Feminist Theological Analysis of the Uses of Religious Symbolism* (Lewiston: N.Y.: Edwin Mellen Press, 1985).

19. Caroline Walker Bynum, *Jesus as Mother: Studies in the Spirituality of the High Middle Ages* (Berkeley: University of California Press, 1982).

20. Ibid., pp. 129–35.

21. Ibid., p. 140.

22. Ibid., pp. 172–85.

23. Ibid., pp. 189-90; 208-9; see also Bynum, "'. . . And Woman His Humanity': Female Imagery in the Religious Writing of the Later Middle Ages," in *Gender and Religion.*

24. Johnson, "The Incomprehensibility of God," p. 456.

25. Ibid., p. 461.

26. Ibid.

27. Ibid.

28. A representative listing of significant recent works of this type would include Merlin Stone, *When God Was a Woman* (New York: Harcourt Brace Jovanovich, 1976); Carl Olson, ed., *The Book of the Goddess: Past and Present* (New York: Crossroad, 1985); Rosemary Radford Ruether, *Mary: The Feminine Face of the Church* (Philadelphia: The Westminster Press, 1977) and *Sexism and God-Talk;* Christine Downing, *The Goddess* (New York: Crossroad, 1981).

29. Stone, *When God Was a Woman,* pp. 1-8, passim; Anne L. Barstow, "The Prehistoric Goddess," in *The Book of the Goddess,* pp. 7-15.

30. Stone, *When God Was a Woman,* pp. 129-52.

31. Ibid., p. xi.

32. Emily Culpepper notes that not all feminists engaged in the recovery of the goddess see themselves as part of a religion, and lack interest in organizing themselves "beyond occasional rituals." See "A Sympathetic Critique," in *Shaping New Vision,* p. 54.

33. Christ, "Why Women Need the Goddess," in *Womanspirit Rising,* pp. 273-87.

34. Ibid., p. 276. See also Culpepper, "A Sympathetic Critique."

35. Culpepper, "A Sympathetic Critique," p. 60.

36. Ibid., pp. 62-68.

37. See Annette Daum, "Blaming Jews for the Death of the Goddess," *Lilith* 7 (1980), pp. 13-14; Judith Plaskow, "Blaming Jews for the Birth of Patriarchy," *Lilith* 7 (1980), pp. 11-13.

38. Culpepper, "A Sympathetic Critique," p. 68.

39. The use of Goddess-worship practices (especially Wiccan) by Christian feminists is impossible to document fully, but I believe it is increasingly common. In "The Feminist Liturgical Movement," Rosemary Radford Ruether notes that at gatherings of Christian women the use of elements from Jewish feminism as well as the Goddess movement has become commonplace; J. G. Davies, *A New Dictionary of Liturgy and Worship* (London: SCM Press, 1986), p. 241.

40. Stone, *When God Was a Woman*, p. 1.

41. Culpepper, "A Sympathetic Critique," p. 54.

42. (Boston: Beacon Press, 1985.)

43. In *Women-Church* Ruether notes the multiple layers of liturgical tradition in Judaism and Christianity and urges the reappropriation of "the hallowing of nature and cyclical time of ancient pre-Judeo-Christian traditions," p. 104. However, she advances a critique against "the pagan feminist movement" as unhistorical and escapist (pp. 105-6). Since she does not in this context cite any representatives of this movement, and since, as already noted, this movement is highly diverse, her critique is difficult to answer. Nevertheless, many of the liturgies included in the book show clear influence from the Goddess movement.

44. See Gerda Lerner, *The Creation of Patriarchy* (New York: Oxford University Press, 1986), pp. 26-35.

45. Charlotte Perkins Gilman, *His Religion and Hers* (Westport, Conn.: Hyperion Press, 1976, reprint of 1923 edition); Ellen DuBois, ed., *Elizabeth Cady Stanton and Susan B. Anthony: Correspondence, Writings, Speeches* (New York: Schocken Books, 1981).

46. Collins, "Naming God in Public Prayer," p. 303.

47. The important distinction between the experience of motherhood and its ideology in patriarchy was made initially by Adrienne Rich in *Of Woman Born: Motherhood as Experience and Institution* (New York: W. W. Norton, 1976). See further, Judith Plaskow, "Woman as Body: Motherhood and Dualism," *Anima* 8 (1981), pp. 56-57.

48. Collins, "Naming God in Public Prayer," p. 303.

49. Rita M. Gross, "Hindu Female Deities as a Resource for the Contemporary Rediscovery of the Goddess," in *The Book of the Goddess*, p. 225.

50. Sallie McFague, *Models of God: Theology for an Ecological, Nuclear Age* (Philadelphia: Fortress Press, 1987), pp. 117-228. McFague also slips into maternalism in her association of mother-love with agapic love and in her equation of women with mothers, p. 100.

51. Ibid., pp. 99-100.

52. Culpepper, "A Sympathetic Critique," p. 65.

53. Rita Gross, "Roundtable Discussion: Feminist Reflections on Separation and Unity in Jewish Theology," *Journal of Feminist Studies in Religion* 2, no. 1 (1986), p. 128. See also Nancy Jay, "Gender and Dichotomy," *Feminist Studies* 7, no. 1 (1981), especially her excellent discussion of the effects of "A, Not-A" thinking, pp. 38-56.

54. Drorah Setel, "Roundtable Discussion: Feminist Reflections on Separation and Unity in Jewish Theology," p. 116.

55. Ibid., p. 117.

56. Ibid., p. 118. On translation of traditional Hebrew prayer-texts, see also Lawrence Hoffman, "Blessings and Their Translation in Current Jewish Liturgies," *Worship* 60 (1986), pp. 134-61; and Marcia Falk, "Notes on Composing New Blessings: Toward a Feminist-Jewish Reconstruction of Prayer," *Journal of Feminist Studies in Religion* 3, no. 1 (1987), pp. 39-53.

57. Johnson, "The Incomprehensibility of God," p. 459.

58. Ibid., p. 458.

59. See Sallie McFague's discussion of this problem in *Models of God*, pp. 166-67, 223.

60. Ibid., p. 184.

61. Ibid., p. 182.

62. For a critique of this formula, see Lawrence Hull Stookey, *Baptism: Christ's Act in the Church* (Nashville: Abingdon Press, 1982), pp. 198-200; Gail Ramshaw-Schmidt, *Christ in Sacred Speech: The Meaning of Liturgical Language* (Philadelphia: Fortress Press, 1986) and "Naming the Trinity: Orthodoxy and Inclusivity," *Worship* 60 (1986), p. 492.

63. Ramshaw-Schmidt, "Naming the Trinity," pp. 491-98.

64. Ibid., p. 496.

65. Collins, "Naming God in Public Prayer," pp. 295-300.

66. McFague, *Models of God*, pp. 182, xii.

67. Ibid., pp. 98-99.

68. Ibid., p. 99.

69. Ibid., p. 100.

70. It is unfortunate that McFague does not discuss the misogyny in classical views on friendship. See Elizabeth Clark, *Jerome, Chrysostom, and Friends* (Lewiston, New York: Edwin Mellen Press, 1979). For a constructive study of female friendship, see Janice Raymond, *A Passion for Friends: Toward a Philosophy of Female Affections* (Boston: Beacon Press, 1986).

71. See Michelle Cliff, "I Found God in Myself and I Loved Her / I Loved Her Fiercely: More Thoughts on the Work of Black Women Artists," *Journal of Feminist Studies in Religion* 2, no. 1 (1986), pp. 7-39; Joseph M. Murphey, "Oshun the Dancer," in *The Book of the Goddess*, pp. 190-201.

72. See Paula Gunn Allen, *The Sacred Hoop: Recovering the Feminine in American Indian Traditions* (Boston: Beacon Press, 1986).

73. For a provocative examination of this image and its implications, see Barbara Walker, *The Crone: Woman of Age, Wisdom, and Power* (San Francisco: Harper & Row, 1985).

74. Collins, "Naming God in Public Prayer," p. 293.

75. Ramshaw-Schmidt, *Christ in Sacred Speech*, pp. 23-26.

76. Adrienne Rich, "The Images."

CHAPTER FIVE

1. The literature on this is vast and growing. Some of the most important and accessible works include: Letty M. Russell, ed., *Feminist Interpretation of the Bible* (Philadelphia: The Westminster Press, 1985); Elisabeth Schüssler Fiorenza, *In Memory of Her: A Feminist Reconstruction of Christian Origins* (New York: Crossroad, 1983), and *Bread Not Stone: The Challenge of Feminist Biblical*

Interpretation (Boston: Beacon Press, 1984); Phyllis Trible, *God and the Rhetoric of Sexuality* (Philadelphia: Fortress Press, 1978), and *Texts of Terror: Literary-Feminist Readings of Biblical Narratives* (Philadelphia: Fortress Press, 1984); Adela Yarbro Collins, ed., *Feminist Perspectives on Biblical Scholarship* (Chico, Calif.: Scholar's Press, 1985).

2. Schüssler Fiorenza, "'Our Right to Choose or to Reject': Continuing Our Critical Work," in Russell, *Feminist Interpretation*, p. 130.

3. Letty M. Russell, "Introduction," *The Liberating Word: A Guide to Nonsexist Interpretation of the Bible* (Philadelphia: The Westminster Press, 1976), p. 14.

4. For example, Lawrence Hull Stookey, in *Baptism: Christ's Act in the Church* (Nashville: Abingdon Press, 1982), devotes several pages to a discussion of the meaning and significance of typology for liturgy (pp. 182-85); but more significantly, a typological method informs the entire book, which is concerned, as he puts it in one chapter, with recovering "our capacity to think biblically' in connection with Christian baptism (p. 93). As the book as a whole shows, "thinking biblically" is equated with typological understanding of scripture.

5. Jean Daniélou, *The Bible and the Liturgy* (Notre Dame, Ind.: University of Notre Dame Press, 1956, 1966), p. 4.

6. For a brief discussion of this process, see Gerhard von Rad, "Typological Interpretation of the Old Testament," in Claus Westermann, *Essays on Old Testament Hermeneutics* (Richmond, Va.: John Knox Press, 1963), pp. 22-24.

7. Ibid., pp. 17-20.

8. Linda Clark, Marian Ronan, Eleanor Walker, eds., *Image-Breaking, Image-Building* (New York: Pilgrim Press, 1981), pp. 48-49.

9. Phyllis Trible, *God and the Rhetoric of Sexuality*, pp. 200-2.

10. Ibid., pp. xv-xvi.

11. Trible, *Texts of Terror*, pp. 93-116.

12. For the complete study of the readings of *The Common Lectionary* see Marjorie Procter-Smith, "Images of Women in the Lectionary," in Elisabeth Schüssler Fiorenza and Mary Collins, eds., *Women: Invisible in Theology and Church* (Edinburgh: T & T Clark, 1985; *Concilium* 183), pp. 51-62. As of this writing, *The Common Lectionary* is under further revision, in part to improve the biblical texts referring to women in biblical history.

13. In *The Common Lectionary*, Proper 25, Year A, pairs Ruth 2:1-13 with Psalm 128: "your wife will be like a fruitful vine'; Proper 26, Year A, has Ruth 4:7-17 with Psalm 127: "Lo, sons are a gift from the Lord. . . . Happy is the man who has his quiver full of them." The lectionary thus imposes its interpretation on a story that might well be read not as a celebration of patriarchal marriage but as an indictment of it. After all, the women in the narrative claims that the child is Naomi's, not Boaz's, 4:17.

14. Procter-Smith, "Images of Women," pp. 56, 58-59.

15. Schüssler Fiorenza, *Bread Not Stone*, p. 115.

16. *Women's Ways of Knowing: The Development of Self, Voice, and Mind* (New York: Basic Books, 1986).

17. Ibid., p. 15.

18. Ibid., p. 18.

19. Ibid., pp. 58-59.

20. Ruether, *Women-Church* (New York: Harper & Row, 1979), pp. 88-91. The minimum essential functions she lists are: liturgical creators, teachers, administrators, community organizers, and spiritual counselors. However, she

also includes in the book the text of a sermon which she preached at a women-church conference (pp. 69-74), so it seems that preaching is not excluded as such.

21. See, for example: *Spinning a Sacred Yarn: Women Speak from the Pulpit* (New York: The Pilgrim Press, 1982); Helen Gray Crotwell, ed., *Women and the Word: Sermons* (Philadelphia: Fortress Press, 1978); Ella Pearson Mitchell, ed., *Those Preachin' Women: Sermons by Black Women Preachers,* Volumes 1 and 2 (Valley Forge, Pa.: Judson Press, 1985).

22. See Elisabeth Schüssler Fiorenza's telling exposition of this point in her response to Walter Burghardt, "From Study to Proclamation," *A New Look at Preaching,* John Burke, ed. (Wilmington, Del.: Michael Glazier, 1983), pp. 43-55.

23. Nikki Giovanni, in an interview by Claudia Tate, in *Black Women Writers at Work* (New York: Continuum, 1983), p. 78. Although I am using the "call-and-response" form as a metaphor for a more general principle of feminist preaching, the form is literally a very important element in the black preaching tradition, in that it recognizes the congregation's authority to participate actively in the sermon. I am indebted to Carol Adams for drawing my attention to this passage.

24. Bernadette Brooten, "Inscriptional Evidence for Women as Leaders in the Ancient Synagogue," *SBL Seminar Papers* 1981 (Chico, Calif.: Scholar's Press, 1981), pp. 1-17.

25. Text in Edgar Hennecke, *New Testament Apocrypha,* volume II, ed. Wilhelm Schneemelcher, trans. R. McL. Wilson (Philadelphia: The Westminster Press, 1964, 1965, 1976), p. 687. See also Elisabeth Schüssler Fiorenza's discussion of this saying in the context of early Christianity in "Word, Spirit, and Power: Women in Early Christian Communities," Rosemary Radford Ruether and Eleanor McLaughlin, eds., *Women of Spirit: Female Leadership in the Jewish and Christian Traditions* (New York: Simon and Schuster, Touchstone Books, 1979), pp. 30-70.

CHAPTER SIX

1. Elizabeth Carroll, "Women in the Life of the Church," in *Women Priests: A Catholic Commentary on the Vatican Declaration,* ed. Arlene Swidler and Leonard Swidler (New York: Paulist Press, 1977), p. 61.

2. See also the frequent references to Galatians 3:27-28 as a foundational theological text for women's authority and leadership in the church throughout *Women Priests.*

3. Helen M. Wright, "Diversity of Roles and Solidarity in Christ," in *Women Priests,* p. 247. See also Margaret Farley, "Beyond the Formal Principle: A Reply to Ramsey and Saliers," *Journal of Religious Ethics* 7 (1979), pp. 191-202.

4. Compare the statement of Juan Luis Segundo: "In short, what is plaguing us is not a crisis over the sacraments but a crisis over *the coherence and meaningfulness of the Christian community.*" *The Sacraments Today* (Maryknoll, N.Y.: Orbis Books, 1974), p. 38.

5. See especially Rafael Avila, *Worship and Politics* (Maryknoll, N.Y.: Orbis Books, 1977, 1981), and Tissa Balasuriya, *The Eucharist and Human Liberation* (Orbis Books, 1977).

6. See Janet Walton, "The Challenge of Feminist Liturgy," *Liturgy* 6 (1986), pp. 5-59.

7. Elisabeth Schüssler Fiorenza, *Bread Not Stone* (Boston: Beacon Press, 1984), p. 7.

8. Rosemary Radford Ruether, *Women-Church* (New York: Harper & Row, 1985), passim; Schüssler Fiorenza, *Bread Not Stone,* p. 7; in *In Memory of Her* (New York: Crossroad, 1983), Schüssler Fiorenza compares women-church to Catholic women's religious communities, pp. 346-47.

9. Ruether, *Women-Church,* p. 64.

10. Schüssler Fiorenza, *In Memory of Her,* pp. 346-47.

11. Ibid.

12. These and other biblical emphases are discussed in James F. White, *Sacraments as God's Self Giving* (Nashville: Abingdon Press, 1983), although he does not describe them as types. Lawrence Hull Stookey, on the other hand, in *Baptism: Christ's Act in the Church* (Abingdon Press, 1982) is more explicit; see his discussion of typology on pp. 182-84.

13. On the role of the arts in liturgy, see *Environment and Art in Catholic Worship* (Chicago: Liturgy Training Publications, 1986).

14. White, *Sacraments,* p. 94.

15. Ibid., p. 96.

16. Balasuriya, *The Eucharist,* p. 6. See also Avila, *Worship and Politics,* for a similar argument from a Latin American perspective.

17. David Power, *Unsearchable Riches: The Symbolic Nature of Liturgy* (New York: Pueblo Publishing Company, 1984), pp. 3, 213-14.

18. Avila, *Worship and Politics,* p. 100.

19. Schüssler Fiorenza, *In Memory of Her,* pp. 205-18.

20. Ibid., p. 236.

21. White, *Sacraments,* pp. 48-49.

22. Aidan Kavanagh, *The Shape of Baptism* (New York: Pueblo Press, 1978), pp. 199-200.

23. Ibid., p. 112.

24. Ruether, *Women-Church,* pp. 126-27.

25. Ibid., p. 128.

26. Ibid., see pp. 59-69.

27. Caroline Walker Bynum "Women's Stories, Women's Symbols: A Critique of Victor Turner's Theory of Liminality," in *Anthropology and the Study of Religion,* Roger L. Moore and Frank E. Reynolds, eds. (Chicago: Center for the Scientific Study of Religion, 1984), p. 109.

28. Schüssler Fiorenza, *In Memory of Her,* p. 346.

29. Schüssler Fiorenza, *Bread Not Stone,* p. 7.

30. There is a vast body of literature concerning women's ordination, arguments for it and against it. Summaries may be found in Anne Marie Gardiner, ed., *Women and Catholic Priesthood: An Expanded Vision* (New York: Paulist Press, 1986); Maureen Dwyer, ed., *New Woman, New Church, New Priestly Ministry* (Rochester, N.Y.: Proceedings of the Second Annual Conference on the Ordination of Roman Catholic Women, 1980); Swidler and Swidler, eds., *Woman Priests;* Emily C. Hewitt and Suzanne R. Hiatt, *Women Priests: Yes or No* (New York: Seabury Press, 1973).

31. Elisabeth Schüssler Fiorenza, "Tablesharing and the Celebration of the Eucharist," in *Can We Always Celebrate the Eucharist?* Mary Collins and David Power, eds. (New York: Seabury Press, 1982), p. 4.

32. Ibid., p. 4.

33. Such communities, however, which tend to have a "low" view of the eucharist often tend to have a correspondingly "high" view of preaching, so

that for women in those traditions the sexism of the church reveals itself in restrictions on and anxiety about women as preachers. Characteristically, whatever a given liturgical tradition deems most central to its character and identity, that activity is forbidden to women.

34. See White, *Sacraments*, pp. 56-57.

35. I Corinthians 11:17-34. See Schüssler Fiorenza, "Tablesharing and the Celebration of the Eucharist," pp. 3-12.

36. See also Schüssler Fiorenza, *In Memory of Her:* "How can we point to the Eucharistic bread and say 'this is my body' as long as women's bodies are battered, raped, sterilized, multilated, prostituted, and used to male ends?" p. 350.

37. White, *Sacraments*, p. 110.

38. Adrienne Rich, "Taking Women Students Seriously," in *On Lies, Secrets, and Silence: Selected Prose 1966–1978* (New York: W. W. Norton, 1979), p. 240.

39. For a convenient summary of the state of the restored catechumenate in the Roman Catholic Church, see Michel Dujarier, *The Rites of Christian Initiation*, trans. Kevin Hart (New York: Sadlier, 1979); and Aidan Kavanagh, *The Shape of Baptism*. Although Protestant churches, such as Episcopalian, Lutheran, Methodist, and Presbyterian, have instituted (or are in the process of instituting) changes in their baptismal rites, none has yet attempted to restore the full catechumenal process as has the Roman Catholic Church.

40. Dujarier, *The Rites of Christian Initiation*, p. 33.

41. Rich, "Taking Women Students Seriously," p. 240.

42. Janet Walton, "Ecclesiastical and Feminist Blessing: Women as Objects and Subjects of the Power of Blessing," in *Blessing and Power*, Mary Collins and David Power, eds. (Edinburgh: T. & T. Clark, 1985), p. 79.

43. Dujarier,*The Rites of Christian Initiation*, pp. 78-79.

44. Schüssler Fiorenza, *In Memory of Her*, p. 346.

45. White, *Sacraments*, pp. 36-42.

46. This phrase is taken from an unpublished speech, "Enabling Women for Power by the Spirit," by Martha Gilmore. Delivered to Church Women United, Dallas, Texas, January 1988.

47. White, *Sacraments*, p. 41. See also White, *Introduction to Christian Worship* (Nashville: Abingdon Press, 1980), pp. 190-91.

48. See Alex Stock, "The Blessing of the Font in the Roman Liturgy," pp. 43-52, and Gabriele Winkler, "The Blessing of Water in the Oriental Liturgies," pp. 53-61, in *Blessing and Power*.

49. Dujarier, *The Rites of Christian Initiation*, pp. 67-69.

50. See Jean M. Higgins, "Fidelity in History," in *Women Priests*, p. 89.

51. See White, *Sacraments*, pp. 54-61.

52. Barbara Andolsen, "Roundtable Discussion: Racism in the Women's Movement," *Journal of Feminist Studies in Religion* 4 (1988), p. 113.

53. Adrienne Rich, "Hunger," in *The Dream of a Common Language: Poems 1974–1977* (New York: W. W. Norton, 1978), p. 13.

54. Ntozake Shange, *for colored girls who have considered suicide when the rainbow is enuf* (New York: Bantam Books, 1981), p. i.

CHAPTER SEVEN

1. I am indebted to Sarah Lancaster for this image.

2. Anne Carr, "On Feminist Spirituality," *Horizons* 9 (1982), pp. 96-103.

3. Adrienne Rich, "The Spirit of Place," in *A Wild Patience Has Taken Me This Far: Poems 1978–1981* (New York: W. W. Norton, 1981), p. 41.

4. Alice Walker, *In Search of Our Mother's Gardens* (New York: Harcourt Brace Jovanovich, 1983), p. xii.

5. Joanmarie Smith, "The Case: A Response," *Religious Education* 80 (1985), pp. 634-43.

6. Ibid., p. 642.

7. Rich, "Integrity," in *A Wild Patience*, p. 9.

8. Rich, "Natural Resources," in *The Dream of a Common Language: Poems 1974–1977* (New York: W. W. Norton, 1978), pp. 64-65.

9. Muriel Rukeyser, "Käthe Kollwitz," *By a Woman Writt*, Joan Goulianos, ed. (Baltimore: Penguin Books, 1973), p. 377.